THE GOLDEN RULES OF CONSTRUCTIVE BI

How often have you heard players say 'Bridge is a bidder's game'? It certainly applies at the top levels of the game today, where the standard of card play is normally so high that most matches are won and lost in the bidding. For us lesser mortals, learning how to avoid impossible contracts is surely better than searching for ways to make them.

Bidding depends to some extent on the agreed system, but underpinning all those methods are standards common around the globe: the Golden Rules. The authors combine experience from both sides of the Atlantic and whether you play Acol, Standard American or a Strong Club system, this book offers plenty for you.

Marc Smith writes a regular column on bidding theory in both *Bridge Magazine* and *Bridge Plus* and hosts the former's monthly Partnership Bidding. His previous works on bidding have won acclaim and he also conducts a monthly Internet bidding competition for the Bridge-Forum on-line teaching school. Julian Pottage provides a perfect foil for Marc, with his sympathies towards more traditional methods similar to those that you might meet at the rubber bridge table. He is also an accomplished bridge writer and teacher.

The format is the same as that used in the earlier books in the *Golden Rules* series, with cases for and against each rule, each one explained using example deals. Whilst the book is aimed primarily at intermediate-level players, there is no shortage of experts who would pick up some useful hints.

by Julian Pottage and Marc Smith
THE GOLDEN RULES OF DEFENCE
THE GOLDEN RULES OF DECLARER PLAY

by Julian Pottage
MASTERPIECES OF DECLARER PLAY

THE GOLDEN RULES OF CONSTRUCTIVE BIDDING

Julian Pottage
and
Marc Smith

CASSELL
IN ASSOCIATION WITH
PETER CRAWLEY

First published in Great Britain 2002
in association with Peter Crawley
by Cassell
Wellington House, 125 Strand, London WC2R 0BB
an imprint of the Orion Publishing Group Ltd

A catalogue record for this book is available
from the British Library.

ISBN 0-304-36217-4

Printed and Bound in Great Britain by
Mackays of Chatham, Kent.

Contents

Acknowledgments

The authors wish to thank the proof-reading team who for this book comprised: Maureen Dennison, John Shergold and Andrew Southwell. Their sharp eyes and ability to look at things from a different aspect dealt with a number of useful points.

We are also grateful to our family, friends and colleagues for their assistance, moral or otherwise, in enabling us to complete the work.

Foreword

In today's frantic world, opportunities to play the game of bridge have become increasingly few and far between. This makes it all the more enjoyable to turn a delay on a lengthy train commute into a few hands with your friends and colleagues. Or maybe you get home late every night and an online bridge club provides your only chance to play. There you might partner someone in a far distant country who speaks little English. Perhaps you are in the happy situation that, after playing bridge casually for many years, you at last have some time on your hands. Whether or not you take the game seriously, it helps if you possess a certain level of understanding about what bids mean and what people will read into yours. Here is where the Golden Rules of bidding help you.

In a number of ways bidding at bridge differs from card play. The partnership and competitive elements come to the fore and bidding offers you more scope to exercise your judgement. The fact that the auction tends to be less cut and dried than the play makes it the more important to know the basic rules. Of course system has a role in this but the principles of, for example, calling no-trumps with a balanced hand and stoppers, or of supporting partner when you like his suit transcend such boundaries.

Between this volume and its companion *The Golden Rules of Competitive Bidding* you will find the basic rules employed by players the world over. As in the works on card play in the series we have covered each rule on a case by case basis and used many practical examples for you to follow. We sincerely hope you learn something useful from this book – we did in preparing it!

Marc Smith
Julian Pottage

January 2002

Rule One: Bid Your Longest Suit

Trumps take tricks. It is as simple as that. You probably learned that you need around 25 high card points (HCP) to make game and something like 33 HCP for a small slam. Fortunately, if you have a good supply of trumps, you may require less high-card strength to take the same number of tricks.

Your side's best 'trump fit' will often be in your longest suit. For your side's longest suit to become trumps, you must bid the suit, often as an initial action. The advice to bid your long suit applies whether you are responding or entering a competitive auction, but we will start with some opening bids.

♠ K 6	YOU	PARTNER
♡ A Q 7 5 3	?	
◇ A J 8		
♣ K J 5		

Playing almost any natural system, the normal opening here is One Heart. Why? You need to find partner with only 3-card support in order to make hearts a playable trump suit. ***Bidding your longest suit can start your hand description.***

♠ 3	YOU	PARTNER
♡ A K 5	?	
◇ A J 9 6 5		
♣ A Q J 2		

You have plenty of high cards and partner might pass your opening bid. If instead he owns the right 8 HCP (the club king and the king-queen of diamonds), you may manage to make a slam. Either way one slight problem arises – the enemy lead first. To score lots of tricks you must first get in. Playing in your side's long trump suit may enable you to restrict the opponents to just one spade trick, even if partner produces no strength in spades. Opening One Diamond gets your suit into the frame. ***Bidding your longest suit can provide a safe place to play.***

♠ Q 5	YOU	PARTNER
♡ 9	?	
◊ Q J 8 6 2		
♣ A K 10 7 3		

Here you possess two equally long suits. You want to be able to suggest each of them in turn as a possible trump suit. It may seem strange, but the most economical way to bid them both comes by starting with the higher-ranking one. Open One Diamond intending to rebid Two Clubs over a major-suit or 1NT response. If need be, you can then stop at the 2-level in either of your suits. This does not apply if you open One Club.

♠ A Q 8 6 5	♠ A Q 8 6 5	♠ A Q J 6 5
♡ 10 7	♡ K 7	♡ K 7
◊ 6	◊ 6	◊ 6
♣ A 10 8 5 2	♣ A J 9 5 2	♣ A K 10 5 2

Note that we did not say *always* open the higher-ranking suit with 5-5. Hands with both black suits constitute a special case. There are those who staunchly advocate opening One Spade, while others resolutely prefer One Club, but we believe that the correct opening bid depends upon the strength of your hand. With a minimum opening, you cannot afford to start with One Club. Imagine the auction goes 1♣-(1♡)-Pass-(2♡)-? Would you now feel comfortable rebidding Two Spades with the first of these hands? What if your right-hand opponent (RHO) jumped to Three Hearts? Opening One Club commits you to bidding spades later, even in the face of enemy bidding.

To open One Club you must be strong enough to bid twice on your own. With the weakest hand above, open One Spade planning to call clubs only if partner responds 1NT. With the middle example you can begin with One Club, aiming to rebid spades twice or compete in them. With still more strength, as in the third hand, you could adopt the same approach. An equally good alternative is to start with One Spade intending to make a high reverse into Three Clubs to show your values and suits that way. ***Bidding your longest suit can prepare you for a rebid.***

```
♠ A 10 6 5      YOU         PARTNER
♡ K J 4         ?
◊ Q 6
♣ A J 9 2
```

This time, you have no 'long suit' as such. Which suit you should open with a major-minor 4-4 (assuming the hand falls outside your range for 1NT) is a matter of style. If you employ a 5-card major system, you must start off with One Club. Playing 4-card majors, you face a choice. A good general rule is that you should open the major with weak hands but the minor on stronger hands.

If you are weak, you only intend to bid once unless partner forces you to speak again. Also, to announce that you have a balanced hand, you intend to make your rebid in no-trumps. So it is important to get your major suit into the auction. You would, therefore, open One Spade intending to pass a 1NT response. With a stronger hand, one on which you expect to bid a number of times, you should allow room to explore all possible strains. With this collection, clubs, spades and no-trumps all appear quite plausible resting spots, but hearts and even diamonds might be right. So, with a bit more, you could open One Club and leave space for partner to describe his hand.

```
♠ K Q 8 5       YOU         PARTNER
♡ K Q 9 3       ?
◊ A Q 6
♣ 7 4
```

Holding two 4-card majors, and assuming you cannot open 1NT, there is no question of which one you should bid first – the lower. If you open One Spade and partner lacks the strength to respond at the 2-level, you will miss a 4-4 or even a 5-4 heart fit as you will pass a 1NT response. Opening One Heart leaves room for partner to bid spades at the 1-level. If you have a fit in either major, you are sure to find it. ***Bidding your longest suit can leave space for partner to respond.***

♠ Q J 9 3   YOU   PARTNER
♡ 5   ?
◇ A K 10 6
♣ K 9 4 2

'Open your longest suit' does not help much this time, does it? With three biddable suits, which should you open?

In the previous example, we saw that you should open the lower of two 4-card majors to facilitate finding a fit in either suit. The same principle applies when holding three 4-card suits. Opening the lowest suit allows you to find a fit in any of them. Partner may raise clubs or he may respond in diamonds or spades. Of course, you expect hearts, your singleton, to be his longest suit, but that need not be the case. If he does respond One Heart, you will still have an easy One Spade rebid.

The traditional rule of opening with the 'suit below the singleton', in this case One Diamond, makes it harder to locate your fit if it happens to be in clubs.

♠ Q 9 8 5   YOU   PARTNER
♡ K Q 9 3   ?
◇ A Q 9 6
♣ 4

Unfortunately, most rules give rise to exceptions. Suppose you follow the rule here and open your lowest 4-card suit, One Diamond. What will you do if partner responds Two Clubs?

When you open the bidding, you should always consider how you will rebid if your partner makes the least convenient response. Here, you might reasonably expect him to respond in your short suit. If your system allows you to rebid 2NT with this strength after a Two Club response, go ahead and open One Diamond. If it does not then you will have to open One Heart. By doing so, you leave yourself room for a Two Diamond rebid over a Two Club response. Partner will tend to place you with a 5-card heart suit for this sequence, but you cannot really help that. *Bidding your longest suit can cater for a response in your singleton.*

		YOU	PARTNER
♠	Q J 9 6 5 2	YOU	PARTNER
♡	Q 6	1♠	1NT/2♣/2◊/2♡
◊	K 10 4	?	
♣	K 3		

Having opened your longest suit, you get a second chance to describe your hand with your rebid. You may think it wasteful to bid your long suit for a second time – after all, your partner already knows about it. This is not so, as the playing strength of a 6-card suit greatly exceeds that of a 4-card suit.

Remember what we said at the start about big trump fits. Suppose partner holds three spades. When you opened One Spade, he may have known only that you had at least a 4-card suit. He could hardly commit to that suit as trumps when you might possess just seven between you. This time you have six spades and as little as a doubleton provides adequate support.

Rebidding Two Spades over a 1NT response promises at least a 6-card suit. Over a Two Club response, it is very likely that you hold six (you do not have four cards in any other suit, and with some sort of 5-3-3-2 you might have opened or rebid 1NT). Over a red-suit response, you might need to rebid Two Spades with a 5-card suit if, for example, you hold four clubs but too little strength to make a reverse bid at the 3-level. Even so, rebidding spades gives easily the best description of this hand. ***Bidding your longest suit can show extra length.***

		YOU	PARTNER
♠	K 8 5	YOU	PARTNER
♡	Q 3	–	1NT (12-14)
◊	K Q 10 6 3 2		
♣	10 4		

Precisely how you bid this hand will depend on your system, but you sure do want to discover if partner has a diamond fit. If partner's diamonds look something like A-x-x, the odds on 3NT sound good. Diamonds will provide six tricks and you will need only three more outside. On the other hand, scoring a no-trump game may well prove impossible if he holds two low diamonds. The opponents may simply kill the diamond suit and you will not have sufficient resources to take nine tricks in the other suits.

Whether you find out about his diamonds by using a jump to Three Diamonds as 'invitational if you have a fit', or you play transfers, or you use Stayman and then a Three Diamond rebid for this purpose scarcely matters. What counts is that you have some mechanism to bid diamonds in a way that invites partner to bid 3NT with fitting cards. *Bidding your longest suit can emphasise where you need help.*

♠ K J 7 5	YOU	PARTNER
♡ 10 6 5	–	1♠
◇ A K J 8 2	?	
♣ 4		

Slam bidding is difficult. You need more than just good trumps – it takes lots of high cards to score 12 tricks. A source of tricks will often enable a slam to make even without great high-card strength. When you pick up a hand such as this, your first reaction should be 'Does partner have any diamond fit?'

Facing ◇ Q-x-x and a stiff heart, this hand offers good slam potential. Opposite ♡ Q-x-x and a singleton diamond, it has none. Tell partner that you own a source of tricks right away so that he can evaluate his hand. You do this by means of what is called 'a delayed game raise'. You start by responding Two Diamonds; on the next round you can tell him that you really like spades, maybe via a Splinter in clubs. First things first – have him focus on his diamonds. *Bidding your longest suit can suggest a source of tricks.*

♠ A Q 9 6 3	YOU	PARTNER
♡ 7 4	1♠	2♣
◇ A Q 8 2	2◇	2♡ (fourth-suit forcing)
♣ 8 2	?	

Partner's fourth-suit Two Heart bid is forcing. Here you must bid something. You have already told him that you hold five spades and four diamonds. This time round your hand contains no particular feature that you wish to stress. Bidding Two Spades simply suggests you have no more descriptive bid available. *Bidding your longest suit can keep the auction alive.*

Sometimes you do not want to keep the bidding going – indeed maybe you have no right to start it in the first place. This brings us to the first case for going against the rule:

		YOU	PARTNER
♠	7 5	?	
♡	Q J 8 6 2		
◇	A 6 3		
♣	K 8 4		

In today's aggressive world this is still not an opening bid in normal methods. It looks close but, as one of the authors used to have to explain regularly to a former partner, 'You are allowed to be maximum sometimes'. Sure, opening One Heart on this hand gets your long suit into play, but partner may hold something like a balanced 13 count. In that case he may very well carry you too high, expecting you to own the values for an opening bid. *Not bidding your longest suit can keep you out of trouble.*

On our next example we presume that you are not using a 16-18 1NT opening – hardly anyone plays it that strong these days as 15-17 rests more easily in most systems and provides a more than ample safeguard against getting doubled.

		YOU	PARTNER
♠	A Q 6 2	?	
♡	K Q 8 3		
◇	10 6		
♣	A K 5		

We have already seen that a One Heart opening is often the right way to get the ball rolling on this type of hand. Correct, that is, if you are playing a system that allows 4-card major-suit openings. Many players prefer to promise a 5-card suit when they open a major, and they would therefore open this hand with a 'prepared' One Club. *Not bidding your longest suit can let you adhere to a 5-card major system.*

On the previous hand, there may have been a reason for bidding a 3-card suit instead of one with four cards. Sometimes it pays to open a 5-card suit rather than a 6-carder.

```
♠ 4                    YOU        PARTNER
♡ Q J 8 7 5            ?
◇ A K 10 6 4 3
♣ 5
```

This is a thorny old problem. Should you open the bidding One Heart? Doing so gives you a comfortable Two Diamond rebid whether partner responds in spades, clubs or no-trumps. Or should you open your longest suit, One Diamond, which although more descriptive in the short term, leaves you with a choice of poor options at your second turn? The choices then lie between rebidding Two Diamonds, concealing your 5-card major, or reversing to Two Hearts, and grossly overstating your strength. It depends partly on personal style, but the 'normal' action would be to open One Heart. In effect you treat the hand as 5-5 in the reds. *Not bidding your longest suit can save you from reversing with a minimum 5-6.*

```
♠ K J 3                YOU        PARTNER
♡ 10 8 6 4 2           ?
◇ A K 9
♣ Q 5
```

Many players are loathe to open 1NT when holding a decent 5-card major. However, a significant body of expert opinion holds that you should open all balanced hands with 1NT if they fall within range, a reasonable 5-card major notwithstanding (you can still locate a 5-3 fit on game hands by using a special version of Stayman that asks for 5-card majors). No matter where you stand in this debate, it seems clear that describing your hand as 'balanced' provides the best option when your longest suit is of very poor quality, as above. If you happen to be playing a weak no-trump (12-14) or perhaps a Precision style (13-15), you should definitely prefer that to a One Heart opening on this collection. *Not bidding your longest suit can work well when its texture is poor.*

The poor quality of your suit was a factor here in deciding not to prefer no-trumps. Oddly enough, having an exceptionally good suit can also provide a reason for doing the same.

```
♠ Q 7            YOU        PARTNER
♡ J 4            ?
◇ A K Q J 10 8 6
♣ 10 2
```

You need quite a lot of goodies to muster eleven tricks. When your long suit is a minor, it will often turn out best to play in the 9-trick no-trump game. Remember that each card can only ever take one trick. Those seven diamond winners can score no more than seven tricks regardless of whether you choose them as trumps. Imagine partner holds something like:

```
♠ J 5 3
♡ A 7 3
◇ 9 7 4 2
♣ A 9 6
```

Although you own an 11-card diamond fit, you can still make only nine tricks with diamonds as trumps – the same nine that you can score in a no-trump contract.

A hand such as this is about perfect for the 'Gambling Three No-trumps'. Using this convention, a 3NT opening bid shows a solid 7- or 8-card minor suit and no outside ace or king. With a smattering of values, partner should pass. *Not bidding your longest suit can get you into no-trumps with a solid minor.*

```
♠ 6              YOU        PARTNER
♡ A J 9 7 4      1♡         1♠
◇ K Q 8 2        ?
♣ K 7 4
```

When we broached the subject of opener's rebid, we explained that repeating your longest suit showed both extra length in that suit and denied holding a second conveniently biddable suit.

Logic therefore suggests that bidding your longest suit is a sub-optimal option here. Playing Standard Acol partner already knows that you hold at least four hearts. By bidding Two Diamonds now, you tell him that you have four cards in that suit and also that you possess a fifth heart. Why?

You would have opened 1♣ on a 1-4-4-4 hand and, with only 4-4 in the reds, you would have a balanced hand and either opened or rebid in no-trumps. *Not bidding your longest suit can spare you from showing the same length twice.*

♠ Q 8 7 5 3 2	YOU	LHO	PARTNER	RHO
♡ 10 6 4	–	1♡	2NT *	Pass
◊ K 6 4	?			
♣ 5				

* Unusual: 5-5 or better in the minors

Are you thinking of bidding your longest suit? If so, then think about one of the basic objectives of bidding – to find a suit in which your side holds at least eight trumps. Partner's Unusual 2NT overcall showed ten or more minor-suit cards. This makes the odds high that he holds fewer than two spades. South might have raised hearts if he had support, and his failure to do so suggests that partner will turn up with a couple of hearts. That leaves little room for many spades, doesn't it?

You already know that your side possesses at least eight diamonds. Partner has asked you to pick one of the minors. Introducing your spade suit in the face of his request shows a much stronger suit than this. *Not bidding your longest suit can be sound when partner has asked for the others.*

♠ 10 2	YOU	PARTNER
♡ J 9 7 6 5 3 2	–	4NT
◊ 10 8 4	?	
♣ A		

Just about every bridge player uses some conventions. Blackwood is one of the most widely used, and this opening 4NT bid is a standard variation that asks you to show what specific aces, if any, you hold.

When answering an ace-asking enquiry such as Blackwood, your response bears no relationship to your length in the suit you bid. In this case, the correct bid is Six Clubs – 'I have the ace of clubs and no other ace, partner.' *Not bidding your longest suit can answer a specific question.*

```
♠ 6              YOU       PARTNER
♡ A K 7          1◇        1♡
◇ A Q 10 8 6 3   ?
♣ A Q 5
```

You have a very good hand and, once partner responds, you intend to reach game. You can hardly just bid game because you cannot be sure in which denomination you want to play. Nor can you rebid your longest suit – both Two Diamonds and Three Diamonds would be non-forcing. You could, perhaps, jump to Four Diamonds, but that may backfire if 3NT is your best spot. Besides, many people play a jump to Four Diamonds as a hand with 4-card heart support and very good diamonds.

On this hand, you will have to invent a suit in which to make a forcing bid, and the logical suit to choose is clubs. Jump to Three Clubs. Partner cannot now pass below game, and you may investigate each of the possible strains in relative comfort. *Not bidding your longest suit can avoid the risk of missing game if partner were to pass.*

```
♠ K 10 7 6 5     YOU       PARTNER
♡ 8 6 4          –         2♣
◇ 10 6 5 2       ?
♣ 3
```

By responding to a 1-level opening bid, you promise some values. With none, you simply pass partner's opening bid.

When partner opens with an artificial strength-showing Two Clubs, you may not pass. Indeed, unless he next rebids 2NT, you must keep responding until your side reaches game. Your first priority when holding a very poor hand is therefore to warn partner that you have little or nothing. You can achieve this via a conventional Two Diamond 'negative response' or denial.

Do not worry that the chance to bid your longest suit will never come. Partner is going to bid again over Two Diamonds. Most likely, you will get to show your spades at your next turn, and you may do so freely having already denied any significant values. *Not bidding your longest suit can permit you to convey weakness via a delayed bid.*

Golden Rule One:

Bidding Your Longest Suit can

. . . Start your hand description;
. . . Provide a safe place to play;
. . . Prepare you for a rebid;
. . . Leave space for partner to respond;
. . . Cater for a response in your singleton;
. . . Show extra length;
. . . Emphasise where you need help;
. . . Suggest a source of tricks;
. . . Keep the bidding alive.

Not Bidding Your Longest Suit can

. . . Keep you out of trouble;
. . . Let you adhere to a 5-card major system;
. . . Save you from reversing with a minimum 5-6;
. . . Work well when its texture is poor;
. . . Get you into no-trumps with a solid minor.
. . . Spare you from showing the same length twice;
. . . Be sound when partner has asked for the others;
. . . Answer a specific question;
. . . Avoid the risk of missing game if partner were to pass;
. . . Permit you to convey weakness by a delayed bid.

Rule Two: Bid No-Trumps with a Flat Hand

As we said in the last chapter: 'trumps take tricks'. It therefore stands to reason that you do not want to choose a trump suit in which you hold barely more cards than the enemy. In this case, you may be better off without trumps, particularly if you have no ruffing values. Besides, no-trump contracts score more than suit contracts at the same level. This can prove decisive at match-point (or board-a-match) scoring, or if the limit on the hand is nine tricks, when 3NT offers the only hope of game.

♠ A 5	YOU	PARTNER
♡ A Q 7 2	?	
◇ 9 8 3		
♣ K 10 8 3		

Precisely how you bid this hand type will depend on your methods, but the key is to bid no-trumps as soon as possible, thus describing the overall balanced nature of your hand.

Playing a weak (12-14) no-trump, you need look no further. Open 1NT. Do not worry that you have one suit containing no honour. With only 12-14 HCP, this happens quite often.

In a strong-no trump position, you should open one of your suits and rebid 1NT. If you are playing 4-card majors and that a non-jump 2NT rebid shows a minimum, you can open 1♡. Otherwise you will have to start with 1♣ and rebid 1NT unless your partner happens to respond in hearts. *Bidding no-trumps with a flat hand can describe your shape and point count.*

♠ K J 6	YOU	PARTNER
♡ K J 8	1◇	1♡/1♠
◇ A Q 7 4	?	
♣ K 10 5		

This hand, with no ruffing values, is even more no-trump oriented than the previous one. Moreover, with tenaces in every suit, you would very much like the lead coming up to your hand.

Playing a strong no-trump, you could describe your hand immediately with a 1NT opening. Using a weak no-trump, you must start with 1◇, but you will rebid in no-trumps over just about anything partner might do. ***Bidding no-trumps with a flat hand can protect your tenaces.***

North–South game
Dealer West

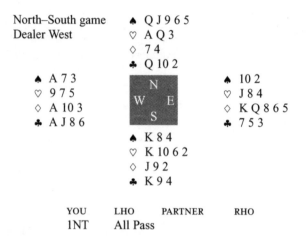

```
              ♠ Q J 9 6 5
              ♡ A Q 3
              ◇ 7 4
              ♣ Q 10 2

♠ A 7 3              N              ♠ 10 2
♡ 9 7 5                             ♡ J 8 4
◇ A 10 3       W           E        ◇ K Q 8 6 5
♣ A J 8 6            S              ♣ 7 5 3

              ♠ K 8 4
              ♡ K 10 6 2
              ◇ J 9 2
              ♣ K 9 4
```

YOU	LHO	PARTNER	RHO
1NT	All Pass		

Observe the pre-emptive effect of your weak no-trump opening on the West cards. North-South have an easy nine tricks in spades (or eight in hearts) but, with their high card strength divided and neither player holding a shapely hand, they cannot get into the auction.

To bid over an opposing 1NT opening, you need either a strong hand (15+ HCP to double a 12-14 1NT for penalties) or some shape (a 6-card suit or a two-suited hand). Depending on what precise methods you use, you might come in with 5-4 shape. With a moderate 5-3-3-2 type, such as this North hand, an overcall would be against the odds.

You can see how much easier things are for your opponents if you open this West hand 1♣. North will come in with a 1♠ overcall and you will record -140 (or 60 below and 30 above at rubber). In 1NT, you can take seven top tricks: +90. ***Bidding no-trumps with a flat hand can prevent a one-level overcall.***

```
♠ Q 10 4        ♠ K J 8 6 5
♡ J 7 3         ♡ 6 5
◇ A 8 3         ◇ 10 9 4
♣ A K 8 2       ♣ Q 7 3
```

YOU	LHO	PARTNER	RHO
1NT	2♡	2♠	

Despite the interference, you still manage to uncover your spade fit. This comes about because partner knew you would hold at least two spades, and quite possibly three or even four.

Life would have been tougher for partner if you had opened 1♣ and LHO came in with a 2♡ overcall. For a start, a 2♠ bid would have been forcing, and his hand looks nowhere near strong enough for that. What is more, he could not guarantee to find you with any spades. ***Bidding no-trumps with a flat hand can indicate at least tolerance for all suits.***

```
♠ A 4           ♠ K 8 6 5
♡ A 10 5 2      ♡ K 7 4
◇ K 8 6 2       ◇ A 4
♣ Q 8 6         ♣ 10 7 3 2
```

YOU	LHO	PARTNER	RHO
1NT	2♠	Double	

On this layout, you open with a weak no-trump and LHO overcalls 2♠. Your partner is ideally placed to make a penalty double. We have just seen that responder to a 1NT opening can compete on a moderate suit because he can count on at least a doubleton opposite. The same argument applies here – partner knows the opponents can hold at most seven trumps.

Moreover, he can also expect your no-trump opening to deliver fair defensive values. Had you opened, say, 1♣ then you might have held something like ♣A-K-Q-x-x-x and a queen outside. Defensively, that hand would offer very little. After the 1NT opening, he knows your high-card values will be fairly well scattered and you will not hold a long suit anywhere. ***Bidding no-trumps with a flat hand can suggest fair defence.***

	YOU	PARTNER	
♠ K 7 3	YOU	PARTNER	♠ Q 10 6 2
♡ Q 6	1NT	2◇	♡ K J 10 9 4
◇ A 10 4	2♡	2♠	◇ 5
♣ Q J 6 5 2	2NT	3♣	♣ A K 4
	3♡	4♡	

With the use of transfers fast becoming widespread, even casual partnerships have available fairly sophisticated methods for responding to a 1NT opening. These will often allow the responder to describe his hand quite accurately at a relatively low level.

In the auction here, you open with a weak no-trump and partner shows first five hearts (with a 2◇ transfer) and then four spades. You announce a minimum opening without four spades or three hearts (with 2NT) and he continues by bidding his third suit, thus pinpointing the diamond shortage. You now know two things: that 3NT is unlikely to be the right game, and that your hearts are very good in context (you denied three on the previous round). You therefore suggest hearts as trumps and, with such good intermediate cards in the suit, your partner happily accepts. *Bidding no-trumps with a flat hand can allow full exploration.*

	YOU	PARTNER	
♠ 8	YOU	PARTNER	♠ A J 7 5 2
♡ 10 8	–	1♠	♡ J 7 4
◇ A 9 7 6 3 2	1NT	Pass	◇ K 8
♣ Q 10 7 3			♣ K J 2

Bidding 1NT does not always indicate a balanced hand. In the auction given above, your response to partner's major-suit opening simply says two things: firstly, that you do not have support for spades and, secondly, that you lack sufficient values to respond at the 2-level.

Quite what you need to respond at the 2-level depends on your methods. Playing Acol with a weak no-trump, a 2-level response does not promise much more than a good 9-count (i.e., a hand prepared to play in game if the opener rebids a game-forcing 2NT, showing 15+).

Some modern British experts adopt a style more akin to the Standard American approach, which requires stronger 2 over 1 responses. Quite how much stronger will depend on whether a 2-level response is played as forcing to 2NT or to game.

Whichever method you prefer, you will hold plenty of hands like the one above – too good to pass but not strong enough to bid a 2/1. The key point is that a 1NT response tends to deny even as much as 3-card support for partner's major. *Bidding no-trumps with a flat hand can deny support for partner.*

We would like to make one more point before leaving the pair of hands above. You are unlikely to make seven tricks in 1NT, but reasonable breaks would allow you to score nine tricks in a diamond contract. How can you get there, though?

Many players feel honour-bound to mention any reasonable 5-card major, as partner did here. However, a growing school of thought today says otherwise. Holding a balanced hand, your partner should open a weak no-trump, if he has one available, despite the 5-card major. In all probability, you could then have removed to a diamond contract at the 3-level (via Stayman or a transfer, depending on your methods).

♠ K J 10 6	YOU	PARTNER	♠ 4 2
♡ 7 5	–	1♡	♡ A J 10 3 2
◇ J 3	2♣	2◇	◇ K Q 10 4
♣ A Q 8 6 2	2NT		♣ K 7

You bypass your 4-card spade suit at your first turn as your hand contains enough strength to bid both suits. Had partner rebid his hearts over your 2♣ response, you would then have continued with 2♠, a responder's reverse, showing your 4-5 shape and at least the values for 2NT – a perfect description!

Partner's 2◇ bid thwarts that plan. Now 2♠ would be 'fourth suit' – you have bid the other three. It would not signify spades at all. Indeed, the immediate message it would send to partner is that you are looking for a spade stopper from him. Instead, you should bid no-trumps, showing adequate cover in the fourth suit, here spades. Note also that 2NT limits your hand. With a queen more, you would jump to 3NT. *Bidding no-trumps with a flat hand can show a stopper in an unbid suit.*

♠ Q J 8 6	YOU	PARTNER	♠ 4 3
♡ 7 3	–	1♡	♡ A K Q 8 4
◇ Q J 9 5	1♠	3♣	◇ K
♣ K 8 7	3NT		♣ A Q J 10 2

Partner announced a very good hand with his jump rebid, but you may have only a working 3-count. For slam purposes, your honours in partner's short suits could be worthless. With so little help from you, it seems inconceivable that your side can make a slam when partner could only open at the 1-level. Bidding 3NT will put the dampers on partner's ambitions beyond game as it warns him of your potentially wasted values.

♠ Q J 8 6	YOU	PARTNER	♠ 4 3
♡ A 3	1NT	3♡	♡ K Q J 8 4 2
◇ Q J 9 5	3NT		◇ K
♣ K 8 7			♣ A Q J 2

Playing transfers, a slightly different situation presents itself here as partner is unlimited. You open a weak no-trump and he jumps to the 3-level – a slam try usually with a good 6-card suit.

Yes, you have at least an 8-card fit, but your partner knows that too. You do not need to raise hearts to say that you hold at least two of them. You already told him that when you opened 1NT. Your first priority is to convey to partner that you own an unsuitable hand for slam. With just one ace and one king in your 12-14 points, you could hardly hold a worse hand. Bidding 3NT warns partner to advance further with caution. *Bidding no-trumps with a flat hand can discourage slam interest.*

♠ K 7 5 2	YOU	PARTNER	♠ A Q 6
♡ Q J 7	–	1◇	♡ 4 2
◇ A 7	1♠	2♠	◇ K Q J 10 2
♣ K 8 6 2	3NT		♣ Q 7 3

In opening 1◇ partner no doubt intended to rebid 1NT over a 1♡ response. When in fact you called 1♠ the low doubleton heart served as a strong deterrent to rebidding in no-trumps.

Quite correctly partner has raised spades with his 3-card support. Now, to offer a choice of games, and in so doing to imply that you hold only four spades, you bid 3NT. With his hand as given, which contains a source of tricks in diamonds and just three spades, he is delighted to pass.

Note that if you open 4-card majors, a 2NT or 3NT rebid after your 1♡ or 1♠ opening was raised to two would carry the same meaning. Again partner might support initially with three trumps and you need to have the mechanism to find your way out of a 4-3 fit. *Bidding no-trumps with a flat hand can warn of having only four cards in your longest suit.*

♠ Q 8 2	YOU	LHO	PARTNER	RHO
♡ 4	–	–	1♣	2♡
◇ K 8 6 5 3	?			
♣ A 7 5 2				

Where is the no-trump call, we hear you ask? Well, if you are using a prepared club you have a problem. You certainly do not want to sell out to 2♡ with a singleton, yet nor can you risk playing in a 4-3 club fit at the 3-level. By contrast, if you know that partner guarantees at least four clubs for his 1♣ opening, you can bid 3♣ in your sleep. *Bidding no-trumps with a flat hand can obviate the need to make nebulous bids.*

♠ K Q 6	YOU	PARTNER
♡ A Q 7 4	?	
◇ Q J 6		
♣ A 10 4		

This is clearly a no-trump type hand but that does not mean that you can simply bid no-trumps. Whether you use a weak or a 15-17 strong no-trump, you cannot open 1NT on this hand. You are too strong.

If you play 4-card majors, you will have to open 1♡ intending to rebid 2NT over just about any response (most Acol pairs play 2NT as 15+ and game forcing after a 2/1). Playing 5-card majors, you are stuck with opening 1♣. *Do not bid no-trumps with a flat hand when you would be out of range.*

♠ K 9 7 3	YOU	LHO	PARTNER	RHO
♡ A Q J 5	–	1♠	3◇ *	Pass
◇ Q 6	?			
♣ J 4 3	* weak			

Quite what you expect from your partner for his weak jump overcall depends to some extent on the vulnerability and your partnership style. Perhaps you envisage ◇A-K-J-x-x-x-x and ♣Q-x. Vulnerable, that sort of combination sounds plausible, and gives you a reasonable shot at nine tricks in no-trumps. In practice, have you noticed that partner very rarely produces the perfect hand? At least, ours seldom seem to do so!

Might he not also have something like ◇K-J-10-x-x-x-(x), the ♡K and a singleton club? You can imagine how the play will then go. The defenders will cash their five club tricks ending on your right and after that the ♠J will be led through your king. You are going to lose at least five clubs, three spades and a diamond – five down. Oh yes, and you have been doubled too.

True, you might manage to make 3NT opposite a suitable maximum with decent breaks. On the other hand, if anything should go wrong, it is all too likely to prove disastrous. ***Do not bid no-trumps with a flat hand when the risk of getting doubled seems too high.***

♠ K 9 3	YOU	PARTNER
♡ A K Q J 4	?	
◇ 10 5 4		
♣ 7 2		

You can take a good idea too far, and this time it matters not what range no-trump you are playing or whether you subscribe to the theory of opening 1NT whenever possible. Holding a distinctly robust 5-card major and two completely bare suits, you should prefer to bid your suit rather than opening 1NT, the 3-5-3-2 shape notwithstanding.

If partner responds 1♠, you will probably be happy to raise to 2♠. If he bids at the 2-level then you can comfortably rebid your hearts. ***Do not bid no-trumps with a flat hand when you hold a pretty decent 5-card major.***

♠ 10 7 4	YOU	PARTNER
♡ J 6	–	1♡
◇ A J 5	2♣	2◇
♣ A Q J 8 4	?	

We saw this auction earlier in the chapter. On that occasion, you held strong spades and we suggested you should bid the appropriate number of no-trumps (depending on your strength).

This time you have a balanced hand, no fit for either of partner's suits and the values to insist on game. Even so, you cannot jump to 3NT because you lack a stopper in the unbid suit. Here you see a classic example of a 'fourth suit forcing' hand. You must bid the fourth suit – 2♠. In essence this tells partner that you own the strength for at least 2NT but that you have no descriptive bid available. If he holds a spade stopper, he will bid no-trumps. If he does not, you probably need to look for an alternative game contract. ***Do not bid no-trumps with a flat hand when you lack a stopper in the unbid suit.***

♠ K 5	YOU	PARTNER
♡ Q J 6 2	–	1♠
◇ A K 8 5	2◇	3♣
♣ Q J 6	?	

Partner has promised extra values with his 3-level reverse. Meanwhile, you have far more than you have shown with your 2-level response. A small slam looks likely and even a grand slam might come into the picture. Give partner something like:

♠ A Q 8 3 2
♡ A
◇ Q 7 2
♣ A K 10 4

6NT is laydown with four clubs, two hearts and three tricks in each pointed suit, and reasonable breaks would allow 7♣ to make. You cannot tell yet what level or strain is best, so use the fourth suit to elicit more information from partner. ***Do not bid no-trumps with a flat hand when slam sounds probable.***

		YOU	LHO	PARTNER	RHO
♠	Q J 9 5	YOU	LHO	PARTNER	RHO
♡	6	–	3♠	4♡	Pass
◊	K 8 6	?			
♣	K J 7 4 3				

If you were told that LHO held long spades and that partner held decent hearts and some values, would you choose to play game in hearts or no-trumps? Holding a double spade stopper that will be wasted in a suit contract and only a singleton heart, you would surely choose the latter. After the auction starts as above, 4NT rates to be at least as good a contract as 4♡. However, you cannot get there – 4NT from you now would no doubt ask for aces (Blackwood). You will just have to pass and hope that partner can come to ten tricks.

		YOU	LHO	PARTNER	RHO
♠	A Q 7	YOU	LHO	PARTNER	RHO
♡	K 5 2	–	–	–	1♠
◊	A Q	?			
♣	K Q 8 7 3				

You cannot have your cake and eat it. Most pairs play some version of the Unusual No-trump convention (whereby a 2NT overcall after RHO's opening shows at least 5-5 in the two lowest unbid suits).

What this means is that you must find an alternative way of describing your hand when you hold a natural 2NT overcall, as here. Not that doing so presents any great difficulty – start with a takeout double and then rebid in no-trumps over partner's response. This sequence shows approximately 19-21 – i.e., a hand too strong for a direct 1NT overcall (which would suggest something like 15-18). *Do not bid no-trumps with a flat hand when doing so would be conventional.*

These two hands provide a prime example of the need to think before you speak (or pull a card out of your bidding box). They also go to show the importance of familiarising yourself with your system. If you have a convention card, it is perfectly fair to use it as an *aide mémoire* in between hands, but not when your turn to bid has arrived.

♠ A 8 6 4	YOU	PARTNER	♠ K 5
♡ 10 7 2	–	1♡	♡ K J 8 6 4
◇ Q 7 5	1♠	2◇	◇ A J 10 8 2
♣ A K 5	?		♣ 2

Your club holding may look like a robust double stopper but, with 3-card support for partner's hearts, you should refrain from jumping to 3NT at this point. You know that partner surely has at least nine red cards, which suggests that one of the black suits will be vulnerable to attack in a no-trump contract. In fact, even though you possess double stoppers in both suits, a club lead threatens to sink the 9-trick game unless the diamond finesse works or you strike lucky in the rounded suits. Now change partner's hand slightly so that he has a low singleton spade. In this case it is plain to see that your ♠A-x-x-x will fail to protect the suit adequately if you need to lose the lead once or twice in order to establish your nine tricks.

On a hand like this one, you do not really want to commit to game in hearts right away, so mark time by bidding the fourth suit (3♣) and see what partner does. When he rebids his diamonds, it will become clear that the suit game is preferable. *Do not bid no-trumps with a flat hand when partner has announced an unbalanced shape.*

♠ Q 10 7 4	YOU	PARTNER
♡ K Q J 6	–	1NT
◇ 5 2	?	
♣ K 8 4		

Partner has shown a balanced hand. Snap! You have one too. Even so, no certainty exists that no-trumps is the correct strain. If partner matches you with four cards in one or other major, it seems quite possible that the suit game (or part-score if his 1NT is minimum and weak) will provide a better spot.

Raising the opening immediately would be precipitous. Start with Stayman (2♣) to find out if you have a 4-4 major-suit fit. *Do not bid no-trumps with a flat hand when partner may have support for your suit(s).*

♠ 7 5 3	YOU	PARTNER
♡ 8 6 4	–	1♣
◇ A 8 7 3	?	
♣ A 8 4		

You could choose to respond 1NT with this hand. Indeed, with many 3-3-4-3 8-counts, that will be the right thing to do. Of course, doing so on this collection risks conceding a positional advantage to the opponents. You derive no benefit from the lead coming up to your hand as you have no tenaces to protect. Conversely, your partner might well hold a tenace or two and thus gain some advantage from becoming declarer.

Simply respond in your longest suit to give partner a chance to rebid in no-trumps. ***Do not bid no-trumps with a flat hand when your partner rates to have tenaces.***

♠ 7 2	YOU	LHO	PARTNER	RHO
♡ A Q 9 2	–	–	1◇	1♡
◇ 8 7 2	?			
♣ A Q J 2				

When you hold a balanced hand you should nearly always bid no-trumps when you are in the right range. People say that the exception proves the rule and this provides a case in point.

You could happily go all the way to 3NT and on a heart lead you would stand every chance of making it. The snag is that a leap in no-trumps conveys the message that you have hearts covered all too well. Your LHO may tune in and decide to attack the unbid major, spades, instead. It costs nothing to bide your time with a simple 2♣ response. You can still bid 3NT on the next round if you feel like it, which you certainly will if partner rebids 2♠. Your pay-off comes if he raises clubs or repeats his diamonds. Then you can call hearts, showing a useful holding in the suit, and asking for further description. This way you can protect any tenuous spade stopper in partner's hand. ***Do not bid no-trumps with a flat hand when your honour strength is highly concentrated.***

Golden Rule Two:

Bidding No-Trumps with a Flat Hand can

. . . Describe your shape and point count;
. . . Protect your tenaces;
. . . Prevent a one-level overcall;
. . . Indicate at least tolerance for all suits;
. . . Suggest fair defence;
. . . Allow full exploration;
. . . Deny support for partner;
. . . Show a stopper in an unbid suit;
. . . Discourage slam interest;
. . . Warn of having only four cards in your longest suit;
. . . Obviate the need to make nebulous bids.

Do not Bid No-Trumps with a Flat Hand when

. . . You would be out of range;
. . . The risk of getting doubled seems too high;
. . . You hold a pretty decent 5-card major;
. . . You lack a stopper in the unbid suit;
. . . Slam sounds probable;
. . . Doing so would be conventional;
. . . Partner has announced an unbalanced shape;
. . . Partner may have support for your suit(s);
. . . Partner rates to have tenaces;
. . . Your honour strength is highly concentrated.

Rule Three: Support Partner

What do you do if you win the lottery or have a birth in your family? Right, you share the good news with your friends and relatives. The same applies when you find a fit in the bidding: you convey the message to partner. Agreeing on a trump suit is one of the two objectives of bidding. Once you have done that, you can concentrate on deciding how high to go. Moreover, if the enemy enter the auction, your partner will be much better placed to compete if he knows that your side has a fit.

Raising partner's suit fosters partnership harmony. Everyone likes to play the hand. Partner will be delighted when you raise his suit since it improves his chances of becoming declarer. Indeed, 'Support partner when you have support for his suit' is one of the most important of all bidding rules.

♠ Q 10 8 5	YOU	PARTNER
♡ 6 4	–	1♠
◇ A K J 7	?	
♣ 9 6 3		

Do not mess around by introducing your diamond suit. Raise spades immediately. If you respond 2◇ for now and express preference for spades later, partner may take a conservative action (such as stopping in a partial or failing to make a slam try) because he is worried about the soundness of the trump fit.

Exactly how you raise spades depends upon your methods. If you play limit raises, this hand looks like a textbook example of a 3♠ bid. It not only tells partner that you have primary support for his suit, it also defines your strength within a fairly narrow range. This makes it easy for partner to judge the subsequent auction.

If you happen to play 'Bergen Raises', or employ a variation of the Jacoby convention whereby a 2NT response shows only at least a sound raise to the 3-level (most people play it as a game force), you should use the appropriate gadget on this hand. ***Supporting partner can show primary support.***

♠ J 10 5	YOU	PARTNER
♡ K	1◇	1♠
◇ A J 8 6 4	?	
♣ Q J 8 3		

Novices tend to shy away from raising their partner with only 3-card support, but this is losing policy. You should feel happy about playing in a 4-3 fit sometimes, certainly at a low level.

On this particular deal partner stands a decent chance of holding at least five spades. The enemy silence suggests they do not possess a huge heart fit, which means partner may hold four hearts. With 4-4 in the majors, he would have responded 1♡, so a 1♠ response will often include five or more spades.

To see why rebidding 2♣ is wrong, ask yourself where you would want to play if partner's hand looks something like:

♠ Q 9 8 4 2
♡ A 7 5 4
◇ 5 3
♣ K 5

Playing in spades, you expect to make three spade tricks, one diamond, and two in each rounded suit – eight. How many tricks will you score in 2◇ after partner gives preference?

Suppose the bidding starts:

YOU	PARTNER
1◇	1♠
2♣	2◇
?	

To bid 2♠ now would indicate a much better hand than this one – something like 16 HCP and the same 3-1-5-4 shape. You would therefore have to pass 2◇. Yuk! You will go down in 2◇ when 2♠ makes easily. Raising to 2♠ at your second turn will please partner and also produce +110 instead of -100.

An immediate raise defines the strength of your hand within a fairly narrow range. Partner will then be well placed to take the right decision. *Supporting partner can limit your hand.*

♠ Q J 7	YOU	PARTNER
♡ 8 4	–	2♣
◊ A 8 7 5 2	2◊	2♠
♣ J 5 3	?	

Despite holding fair values, it is surely right to respond 2◊ at your first turn. Jumping to 3◊ on this month-eaten suit hardly appeals and responding 2NT risks wrong-siding the declaration if no-trumps proves to be the right strain.

After hearing partner's 2♠ rebid, do you feel tempted to bid 3◊? If so, reflect on what you would bid with this hand:

♠ 7	YOU	PARTNER
♡ 8 6 4	–	2♣
◊ J 8 7 5 4 2	2◊	2♠
♣ 9 5 3	?	

You would bid 3◊ at this point, would you not?

To make the same bid on the superb hand that contains primary support for partner's spades just muddies the waters. You can never envisage playing the hand in diamonds, so why waste your breath mentioning the suit? Raise to 3♠ directly, letting partner in on which suit is going to be trumps. After that you can both focus your attention on finding the right level, be it game, slam or even grand slam.

♠ J 10 7	YOU	PARTNER
♡ A K 4	1◊	2♠
◊ A Q 10 5 3	?	
♣ 6 2		

After partner's strong jump shift response, slam (and maybe a grand slam) sounds probable. You have super controls, good trump support, a possible source of tricks and a ruffing value. So you want to leave the maximum room to investigate slam. Do not waste space whilst creating confusion over the issue of which suit should be trumps by bidding 3◊. Tell partner now that spades looks like a good trump suit. Raise to 3♠ and let the cue-bidding begin. *Supporting partner can set the suit.*

	YOU	PARTNER
♠ A K J 4	1◇	1♡
♡ Q 10 6	1♠	1NT
◇ A J 8 7 2	?	
♣ 4		

'Do not keep bidding suits on a balanced hand,' is a saying you may sometimes hear. One of the reasons for sticking to this sound advice is that partner will gain an accurate picture of your hand when you do call three suits.

Bidding 2♡ in the auction shown gives partner an excellent idea of what you hold – five diamonds, four spades and, now, three hearts. This sequence also indicates a non-minimum opening bid. Do you understand why? With the same shape and less high-card strength, say a low spade rather than the king, you would have raised him to 2♡ at your second turn (accepting the slight risk that you may end up in a 4-3 heart fit even when you each have four spades). *Supporting partner can describe your hand pattern.*

Bidding two suits usually indicates at least 5-4 shape. Even playing four-card majors, if you open 1♡ and rebid 2♣/2◇ over partner's 1♠ response, you promise a fifth heart. Can you see why this time? With a balanced hand, you would have opened or rebid in no-trumps. (Yes, you may sometimes need to break this 'rule' when you are dealt certain 4-4-4-1 shapes.)

	YOU	PARTNER
♠ 6 2	1♡	2◇
♡ A J 10 5 3	3◇	
◇ K 9 8 6		
♣ A 4		

The same principle often applies when you raise partner's suit. In the auction here, your raise to 3◇ shows a minimum opening bid and is non-forcing. It also tends to suggest a 5-4 shape (holding eight red cards and 3-2 in the blacks you might have bid no-trumps somewhere along the line or rebid 2♡).

A number of implications follow from this. Firstly, partner can continue with an invitational 3♡. Furthermore a raise by him to 4◇ can be used as a slam try (some people play it is as RKCB), negating the need to jump around on a good hand.

♠ K J 9 8 4	YOU	PARTNER
♡ Q 10 6 2	–	1♢
♢ Q 5	1♠	2♡
♣ 8 2	3♡	

Since partner is unlikely to hold more than four hearts (his second suit), you must hold 4-card support for your raise. If you had just four spades, you would have responded 1♡ rather than 1♠. Hence you have shown five spades by raising hearts. ***Supporting partner can imply extra length in your suit.***

♠ K 7	YOU	PARTNER
♡ A K 8 6 4	1♡	1♠
♢ 7 3	2♣	2♠
♣ K J 10 2	3♠	

When partner rebids his spades, he surely announces at least a 6-card suit but he does not promise any more than a minimum response in terms of high cards. Although you have only 14 HCP, you are well worth a game try – you need partner to hold something like ♠A-Q-x-x-x-x and the ♣Q to make 4♠ an excellent contract, and plenty of other hands will leave it a fair proposition. ***Supporting partner can invite game.***

♠ 9 6	YOU	PARTNER
♡ A 4 2	–	1♠
♢ K Q 8 6 4	2♢	3♠
♣ A J 5	?	

Partner's jump rebid announces at least a 6-card suit as well as extra values. This leads you to think in terms of slam. Much will probably depend on just how solid his spades are. Consider these two possible hands for partner:

♠ K Q 7 5 4 2	♠ A Q J 10 8 4 2
♡ K 5	♡ K 7
♢ A 3	♢ A
♣ K Q 7	♣ 10 6 4

Opposite the first of these hands, you will need some luck in trumps to make 6♠. By contrast, with the second, the small slam is very good and the grand on little more than a finesse. The solution is to jump to 5♠. The fact that you have neither cue-bid a control nor asked for aces means that you are not worried about those things. You simply want him to bid six if he has better trumps than he might have. *Supporting partner can ask him to bid a slam with good trumps in context.*

		YOU	PARTNER
♠	J 8 6 5	Pass	1♠
♡	6	?	
◇	Q 10 7 5 3		
♣	10 6 4		

Although you lack the ordinary high-card strength needed for a response, to some extent point-count goes out of the window when you find a good fit.

If partner had opened 1♡, you would have passed. When he opens a suit in which you possess primary support, passing would constitute a serious error. For a start, do you really want to let the opponents in cheaply to find their heart fit?

In most systems, you would have to content yourself with a simple 2♠. On the other hand, if you happen to be playing Bergen raises, you can jump to 3♠ as a pre-emptive bid. This is exactly the hand on which you should unleash that weapon. *Supporting partner can keep the opponents out.*

		YOU	LHO	PARTNER	RHO
♠	7 5	Pass	Pass	1♡	1♠
♡	J 10 4	?			
◇	6 3				
♣	A Q 9 7 6 4				

Here you can guess the hand on your left is about to raise spades. So you want to choose a bid that leaves some future options. As a passed hand you might consider a non-forcing 2♣ bid if partner's opening bid shows only a 4-card heart suit. Nevertheless, it is still better to raise hearts. This way, having limited your hand and promised heart support, you may be able to offer 3♣ as an alternative contract at your next turn to speak. *Supporting partner can prepare you for the next round.*

♠ J 6 2	YOU	LHO	PARTNER	RHO
♡ Q 7 5	–	–	1♡	2♢
♢ 8 6	?			
♣ A 9 7 6 3				

It matters not whether you are playing four-card or five-card majors. This hand clearly warrants a 2♡ bid. If you still feel less than comfortable raising without four trumps, ask yourself what you would rather bid on this deal. You cannot make a negative double – you lack either the values or spades for that. For sure a forcing bid of 3♣ is totally out of the question, so what else remains? If you pass, what would you propose to do when LHO raises to 3♢ and that gets passed back to you? Pass again…? If so, you should stop reading a book about bidding and pick up one on defensive play, as that is what you must spend most of your time doing.

Passing throughout on a hand such as the one here allows the opponents to steal you blind. Bid 2♡ on the first round, showing your meagre values and the heart support, and leave the rest to partner. He will be suitably placed to decide if you should defend 3♢, compete to 3♡, or perhaps go to game. *Supporting partner can let your side compete effectively.*

♠ K 10 4	YOU	LHO	PARTNER	RHO
♡ J 9 6	–	–	1♡	3♣
♢ K Q 5 3 2	?			
♣ 4 2				

At the 3-level, maybe you feel on shakier ground raising with only three trumps, but what else can you do? If you pass, do you really expect partner to bid again when 3♣ comes around to him if he is looking at something like a 3-5-2-3 16-count? Sure, you might beat 3♣ by a trick or two, but that will provide small compensation for the ten or eleven tricks you could have scored in a heart game. *Supporting partner can get you to a good game or slam contract.*

On the last few hands, the opponents have been bidding. You will find this often happens if you like partner's suit. When one side has a fit, the other side normally has one too.

	YOU	LHO	PARTNER	RHO
♠ 5	YOU	LHO	PARTNER	RHO
♡ Q 9 7 6 5	–	–	1♡	Pass
◊ K J 7 2	?			
♣ 8 5 3				

On this example, the right answer depends a bit on whether partner's opening bid shows five and who is vulnerable. Some of the time, 3♡ will do the hand justice. However, if you are playing 5-card majors and the vulnerability rests in your favour, you should pre-empt to the maximum – 4♡. The odds are high that LHO has spades. If he also holds a decent hand, you must make it as difficult as you can for him to enter the auction. All is not necessarily lost even if LHO comes in with a spade bid over your 4♡. After all, partner might sit there waiting to wield a big penalty double. Alternatively, the opponents may find it hard to judge that they have a slam. They may also look for slam and find the 5-level too high for them.

If they do alight in the right contract, at least you can take heart from the fact that you made things as tough as possible for the enemy by using up their bidding space. **Supporting partner can jump the bidding.**

♠ A 7 5	♠ K J 8 6 2
♡ 10 7 3	♡ 6 2
◊ 7 6 2	◊ K J 9 3
♣ J 9 6 2	♣ K 4

YOU	LHO	PARTNER	RHO
–	1♡	1♠	2♡
2♠			

Although you have an awful lot of losers, there is a good case for bidding 2♠. If the opponents bid on, and especially if they go to game, a spade lead is almost certainly the best start for the defence. If you fail to support his spades, partner may lead something else, perhaps with disastrous consequence. **Supporting partner can encourage him to lead the suit.**

Thus far we have always obeyed the supporting partner rule. Now the time has come to see why you might break it.

♠ J 8 6	YOU	PARTNER
♡ 9 3	–	1♠
◇ K 10 4 2	?	
♣ 10 7 5 3		

You can take a good thing too far. If you had a fourth spade, or possibly a singleton heart, we might recommend a raise to 2♠. On the actual hand, this has too little going for it. What inevitably happens if you do raise on this type of hand is that partner holds a good hand and bids game (or at least make a try for it) and goes one or two down.

You can still come back into the auction if you pass at this juncture. Suppose it continues along these lines:

YOU	LHO	PARTNER	RHO
–	–	1♠	Pass
Pass	Double	Pass	2♡
?			

You should now bid 2♠. This lets partner know that you have a very weak hand with some spade support. He will not get carried away. If in practice LHO takes the push to 3♡, partner will then be able to compete further when he judges it correct so to do. *Do not support partner when your hand is too weak.*

♠ K Q 6 2	YOU	PARTNER
♡ 9 6 3	–	1◇
◇ 10 8 7 5	1♠	
♣ K 6		

If partner had opened your 4-card major, you would raise without hesitation. In contrast, when he opens a minor suit for which you possess primary support, you should investigate potential major-suit fits before supporting the minor. Partner could easily hold four spades and five diamonds. If this is a game hand, you probably want to play in the major suit – after all, it usually proves easier to make ten tricks than eleven. *Do not support partner when higher-scoring strains beckon.*

♠ K Q 7 5	YOU	PARTNER
♡ A 2	–	1♠
◊ A Q J 6 4	?	
♣ 6 3		

With such strong support for partner's major, it is usually right to raise him straight away. Just how many spades would you propose bidding on this hand, though?

Remember that a raise, like a no-trump bid, limits your hand within a fairly narrow range. This hand is far too strong to limit at this stage of the auction.

Some people play 2NT as a game-forcing spade raise and we agree that is an option of sorts here. However, if you start that way, you can never get across your good diamond suit.

Indeed, since a slam seems distinctly possible, you should begin describing your hand with the aim of a slam investigation in mind. Think about the various factors needed to make a slam. A good trump suit is essential, and it is vital that the opponents cannot cash two quick winners; you also require the material to generate twelve tricks, and your potential source of tricks in diamonds could prove decisive for that. Ideally, you want to tell partner that you have slam interest with first-rate spade support, a useful diamond suit, a control in hearts and nothing much in clubs. If you could get all of that across, he would be in a great position to pick the best contract.

Well, how about this auction:

YOU	PARTNER
–	1♠
3◊	3♠
4♡	

An important principle that has become widely established in recent years is to jump-shift with a two-suited hand only when your suits include the one already bid by partner. As you would not, therefore, have called 3◊ with a big red two-suiter, your 4♡ call is a cue-bid agreeing spades.

There, you have done it – you have shown slam interest (a jump shift and a cue-bid), a good diamond suit, spade support, a heart control and no primary club control. You managed all that in just two bids. Surely that is much better than just raising spades to some random level at your first turn. *Do not support partner when this would wrongly limit your hand.*

♠ K 6	YOU	PARTNER
♡ 9 7 5	–	1♠
◇ J 10 2	?	
♣ K 8 7 6 5		

Three or four deals back, you may recall that we suggested you might raise partner's suit to encourage him to lead it. This time around a couple of key differences arise. Firstly, although you have a high spade and an opening lead in the suit would probably serve your side well, a direct raise on a doubleton could lead partner astray in the auction. He may simply bid too much or, if he has a very good hand, choose the wrong game. Secondly, if the auction becomes competitive, he might well over-compete expecting to find a better fit with you.

A desire to direct the lead may take precedence over other factors if LHO seems set to become declarer, but nothing here would indicate this. Simply respond 1NT on this hand. *Do not support partner when you hold insufficient trumps.*

♠ Q J 7	YOU	PARTNER
♡ 10 8 2	–	1♡
◇ J 10 9 4	?	
♣ K 10 2		

In this chapter we have emphasised that you should freely raise a major to the 2-level with 3-card support, as responder and also as opener. As with most rules, exceptions crop up. Facing a 1♡ opening, whether you are playing 4-card or 5-card majors, a 1NT response should work best on this hand. It has no ruffing value and slow stoppers in the outside suits. *Do not support partner when you lack ruffing values.*

	YOU	PARTNER
♠ K Q 4		
♡ 7 3	1NT (12-14)	2♣
◇ A J 8 6	2◇	2♠
♣ K 10 7 3	?	

Using standard methods, partner has announced at least five spades and four hearts. Having already denied four spades with your negative response to Stayman, you have excellent support for spades – so you should raise, right?

Wrong. You limited your hand with your initial bid and now partner wants to sign off at the 2-level. For all you know, he may be looking at a Yarborough. ***Do not support partner when you have already bid your hand.***

Often you face a choice between supporting partner and rebidding your own suit. Compare the next two hands:

	YOU	PARTNER
♠ A K 2		
♡ 6	1♣	1♠
◇ A J 4	?	
♣ 8 7 5 4 3 2		

You hold three trumps, a ruffing value and a minimum opening bid – a combination that strongly suggests raising partner's suit to the 2-level. Make a simple raise to 2♠.

	YOU	PARTNER
♠ 5 3 2		
♡ K Q J 10 9 5	1♡	1♠
◇ A J 4	?	
♣ 6		

This hand contains a number of the same features, but now the raise is markedly inferior. With a suit this solid, you are happy to play in hearts even opposite a shortage. By contrast, a spade contract could prove unmanageable. Partner may hold a suit such as ♠Q-10-x-x – remember, as you opened 1♡, spades was the only suit he could respond in at the 1-level. This increases the chance of his holding just four spades. ***Do not support partner when your suit should play better.***

		YOU	PARTNER
♠	10 6 4	1♣	2♠
♡	K J	?	
◇	A Q 9 2		
♣	K Q 8 2		

Even at the rubber bridge table, a strong jump shift response is almost always based on at least a 5-card suit, and usually longer. So you could raise spades directly. Happily there will be plenty of time for that later. First say to partner that you have a flat hand by rebidding 2NT.

A number of other benefits may come from rebidding 2NT. Firstly, doing so leaves partner room at the 3-level to show if his jump shift was based on a good club fit, by rebidding 3♣. In effect, 2NT is a waiting bid which allows partner room to describe his hand further. Moreover, if this is a slam hand, which seems quite likely, then it may be important to protect your heart holding. By getting in no-trumps now, you enable partner to suggest that strain later without wrong-siding the contract.

		YOU	PARTNER
♠	A Q 10 4	1♠	2♡
♡	Q 10 7	?	
◇	K 9		
♣	A 8 3 2		

A 2♡ response promises at least a 5-card suit. Your heart support thus suffices for an immediate raise. However, doing so would imply a more shapely hand.

Most pairs playing modern Acol treat a non-jump 2NT rebid as a force to game, with a minimum of 15 HCP. If that weapon is available to you, it offers the best way to proceed on this hand. Having already shown a balanced hand, you can support hearts later. For example, if partner raises 2NT to game, you can then correct to 4♡. This way he will work out that you hold a strong balanced hand with 3-card heart support. In auctions where you raise hearts directly, he will expect more distribution. ***Do not support partner when the chance arises to show your hand type at a low level.***

♠ A Q J 7	YOU	PARTNER
♡ K 10 7 3	–	1◇
◇ J 8 6	1♡	2♣
♣ 4 2	?	

By jumping to 3◇, you could express the nature of your hand – an 11-count with 3-card or better diamond support. However, with such strong spades and an essentially balanced hand, 2NT is a much more descriptive choice. This shows the same values as would 3◇, but lets partner know that he need not worry about spades. Since an 11-trick game seems far away, this information should prove far more useful than news of diamond support. Indeed, given that so many of your values lie in the majors, you only envisage playing in a minor if partner has a lot of shape. He still has room to indicate that over 2NT. *Do not support partner when you own a strong holding in the unbid suit.*

For quite different reasons sometimes you must be wary of supporting partner when your side is outgunned. You need to consider whether the prospective benefits from taking action outweigh the potential risks. We conclude the chapter with three variations on this theme.

♠ J 8 6 5	YOU	LHO	PARTNER	RHO
♡ 10 6 5	–	1◇	1♠	2♡
◇ 4 2	?			
♣ 9 7 5 3				

With both sides vulnerable, you can hardly go jumping around on this shapeless hand, 4-card support for partner notwithstanding. You could raise to 2♠, but what do you hope to accomplish by that? You do not want partner to compete further and absolutely no chance exists of buying the contract at the 2-level. All raising does is convey to the opponents that you have a spade fit. If one of them holds, for example, three or four low spades, he will then deduce that his partner is short in the suit. *Do not support partner when doing so would only help the enemy judge their fit.*

♠ 9 6 4	YOU	LHO	PARTNER	RHO
♡ K Q 10 3	–	1◊	1♠	2♡
◊ J 8 6 2	?			
♣ 7 4				

On this deal your opponents alone are vulnerable, which creates an equally good reason for keeping silent. Suppose you bid 2♠ and LHO jumps to 4♡. What do you think that partner will do when he holds a fair 6-card spade suit and a singleton heart? Right, he will save in 4♠ – this is just what you wanted! Few things in bridge are more costly than a phantom sacrifice. Partner will not enjoy going for 500 or so in 4♠ doubled when he sees from the moment dummy hits the deck that you could have defeated the enemy contract.

Raising to 2♠ on this hand invites a disaster. Nothing good can come of it. *Do not support partner when you want to avoid encouraging him to sacrifice.*

♠ 8 7 2	YOU	LHO	PARTNER	RHO
♡ 6 3	–	–	Pass	Pass
◊ Q 8 2	Pass	1♡	1♠	2♡
♣ K J 10 9 4	?			

Given that you hold only six points and partner passed as dealer, there is no chance of outbidding the opponents. LHO owns a good hand and is about to bid game, or at any rate make a try for it. What do you think will happen in you bid 2♠ now? Right, partner will lead a spade against 4♡. Is that what you want?

A spade lead may be right, but then partner probably has a suit that includes the ace-king or king-queen-jack. In those cases he will lead one whether you pass or bid. What you want to avoid is to encourage him to lead from a broken suit headed by the ace-queen or king-jack. If that is his spade holding, you would rather he led a minor suit, or perhaps a trump. *Do not support partner when you might like him to lead some other suit.*

Golden Rule Three:

Supporting Partner can

. . . Show primary support;
. . . Limit your hand;
. . . Set the suit;
. . . Describe your hand pattern;
. . . Imply extra length in your own suit;
. . . Invite game;
. . . Ask partner to bid a slam with good trumps in context;
. . . Keep the opponents out;
. . . Prepare you for the next round;
. . . Let you compete effectively;
. . . Get you to a good game or slam contract;
. . . Jump the bidding;
. . . Encourage him to lead the suit.

Do not Support Partner when

. . . Your hand is too weak;
. . . Higher-scoring strains beckon;
. . . This would wrongly limit your hand;
. . . You hold insufficient trumps;
. . . You lack ruffing values;
. . . You have already bid your hand;
. . . Your suit should play better;
. . . The chance arises to show your hand type at a low level;
. . . You own a strong holding in the unbid suit;
. . . Doing so would only help the enemy judge their fit;
. . . You want to avoid encouraging him to sacrifice;
. . . You might like him to lead some other suit.

Rule Four: Respond up the Line

The opening bidder does not claim a monopoly on identifying the partnership's best suit. Quite often this honour falls to the responding hand.

Like opener, responder usually starts by bidding his longest suit, although sometimes that is impractical. For example, if opener's suit ranks above yours but you lack sufficient strength for a 2-level response, you will be forced to respond 1NT or a suit at the 1-level. This may mean bidding a 4-card suit when you hold a longer one elsewhere.

In this chapter, we will carefully explore responding with suits of equal length. Suppose you hold four cards in each major and partner opens 1◇. Even when your spades are stronger than your hearts, you should still respond 1♡. This is called 'bidding suits up the line'.

The principal reason for bidding your cheapest suit is that your side's best fit may lie in that suit. If you bypass a suit, partner will tend to assume you have fewer than four cards in it. He might not, therefore, introduce such a 4-card suit himself.

Another reason for responding up the line is that partner may be concerned about stoppers in a particular suit for no-trump purposes. Bidding that suit will alleviate his fears somewhat.

♠ Q 9 6 5	YOU	PARTNER
♡ 6 4	–	1♡
◇ K Q J 7		
♣ 7 4 2		

You have enough values to keep the bidding open. Should you respond 1♠ or 1NT? The latter option appears attractive for a number of reasons. Firstly, your hand is balanced, which makes calling no-trumps an accurate description. Secondly, 1NT is a limit bid (showing about 6-9 HCP) and it is a sound principle of bidding to limit your hand as quickly as possible.

However, you should be very wary of bypassing a 4-card major. Partner could hold something like the hand on the next page:

		YOU	PARTNER
♠	K J 10 7	YOU	PARTNER
♡	A K 9 2	–	1♡
◇	A 8 3	1NT	3NT
♣	A 3		

Sure, 3NT might make. The defenders may miss the club lead. Even if they do find it, their clubs might break kindly. By contrast, success in 4♠ depends on much less. The defenders' cards would have to lie extremely poorly for that contract to fail.

Needless to say, if you bypass spades, partner will take for granted that you have neither four spades nor primary heart support. He will therefore proceed directly to what he expects to be the best game contract – 3NT. Besides, he cannot reverse into 2♠, since that would promise 4-5 or better in the majors.

We agree your spades seem relatively poor, but it is still your job to suggest them as a possible trump suit. *Responding up the line can allow you to find a major-suit fit.*

		YOU	PARTNER
♠	K 4	YOU	PARTNER
♡	K J 8 7	–	1♣
◇	A Q J 6 5	?	
♣	10 2		

Scoring 10 tricks usually proves easier than scoring 11, so finding major-suit fits is a primary objective of bidding. Indeed, sometimes you should ignore a minor suit in favour of showing your major. However, it is easy to follow this concept too far.

Once partner opens the bidding, you immediately know with this hand that you will bid game and even a slam is possible. Since the auction should keep going for several rounds, you need not rush to get in your major. With good hands, you should look to describe your whole hand.

Here, your biggest asset is the strong diamond suit. The more moderate 4-card heart suit represents only a secondary feature. By responding 1◇ now, you can introduce your hearts on the next round. Partner will know both that you have a good hand and that you are at least 4-5 in the two suits. *Responding up the line can enable you to describe your hand.*

♠ K 10 6 5	YOU	PARTNER
♡ 7 6 3	–	1♢
♢ 4	1♠	
♣ A Q 8 4 2		

On the previous example, you managed to show both of your suits because you were strong enough to bid twice. This hand illustrates the flip side to that coin. No matter what you set as the systemic threshold for a change of suit response at the 2-level, you can ill afford to respond in clubs on this hand.

Let us suppose for the moment that you respond 2♣. Now imagine partner simply repeats his diamonds. Clearly, you are too weak to reverse into 2♠ facing what sounds like a minimum opening. You would therefore have to pass, leaving partner to toil away in 2♢.

Worse news could still be to come – your partner may have a 4-card spade suit too. As responder, if your hand is worth only one bid, you can hardly ever afford to show a minor if it means bypassing a 4-card major. *Responding up the line can let you show a vital feature at the one level.*

♠ K Q 8 6	YOU	PARTNER
♡ Q 10 5 2	–	1♣/1♢
♢ 6 3	1♡	
♣ J 7 4		

When you have two equal-length suits, bidding them in the natural order should allow you to uncover a 4-4 fit in either suit. If you were to respond 1♠ on this hand, partner would need reversing values in order to mention a heart suit. True, if he rebids his minor or continues with 1NT, you could introduce hearts yourself. However, doing so would risk misdescribing the hand on two counts – making a second bid may overstate your strength, and bidding your majors in this way unquestionably promises at least a 5-card spade suit.

Let's see how much easier things are if you respond 1♡. If you have a 4-4 heart fit, partner will raise your suit. If you have a 4-4 spade fit, he can bid that suit at his second turn. He does not need any extra strength to call spades at the 1-level.

If partner just rebids his minor over 1♡, you can safely pass in the knowledge that you lack any worthwhile fit in a major.

♠ J 2	YOU	PARTNER
♡ 8	–	1♡
◇ K J 9 7 4	?	
♣ K J 9 7 4		

The respond up the line rule can also extend to 5-card suits, certainly in Acol at least. You need to ask yourself the following question: are you worth a second bid if you bid one of your minors and partner rebids 2♡? Clearly, the answer is 'No'. To give yourself the maximum chance of finding a fit in either minor, you should bid your suits upwards – respond 2♣.

Suppose partner's hand looks something like this:

♠ 9 6	YOU	PARTNER	YOU	PARTNER
♡ A K 9 5 2	–	1♡	–	1♡
◇ 8 3	2♣	3♣	2◇	2♡
♣ A Q 6 3	Pass		Pass	

Would you rather play these hands in 2♡ or 3♣? No doubt, you would much rather play in your 9-card fit.

By responding 2◇, you rule out any hope of finding the club fit with partner's actual hand – to do so, someone would have to make an enormous overbid and in that case you would get too high. Responding 2♣ should work equally well when your fit is in diamonds . . .

♠ 9 6	YOU	PARTNER
♡ A K 9 5 2	–	1♡
◇ A Q 8 3	2♣	2◇
♣ 6 3	3◇	Pass

On the second round of bidding you have to content yourself with a single raise. Although your trump support looks very good, the singleton in partner's first suit and the absence of aces both suggest caution. *Responding up the line can allow space to find a fit in a third suit at a suitable level.*

	YOU	PARTNER
♠ 8 4	YOU	PARTNER
♡ 10 6 2	Pass	1♠
◇ K Q 9 7 5	2◇	
♣ A J 2		

When partner opens in third seat he does not promise a rebid. He might open a bit light to suggest the lead or to make life difficult for the enemy. Or he could choose to open a 4-card major in preference to a prepared club, intending to pass your response. If partner might start with one of a suit on a balanced 15-16 then you cannot afford to respond 1NT. You would stand a serious risk of missing game if you did, as he would have no reason to raise. In any event you should feel happy to describe your hand as nearly maximum for your initial pass.

One point to watch for playing match-point pairs is that if you have 3-card support for partner's major (as would be the case if he had said 1♡) you must watch out for the possibility of being left in a lower-scoring strain. Indeed some expert pairs play that a 2-over-1 by a passed hand promises three cards in the suit opened. However, it is only practical to adopt that treatment in conjunction with a 14-16 or 15-17 1NT opening – otherwise you would be stuck with this hand. *Responding up the line can offer a sensible spot when you are a passed hand.*

	YOU	PARTNER
♠ 8 6	YOU	PARTNER
♡ Q 9 3	–	1♠
◇ 10 8 4 2	?	
♣ Q 7 5 3		

All systems include some forcing opening bid such as the 2♣ opening in Acol or Standard American. Partner's failure to wheel out your system strong bid means that he cannot see game in his own hand (or something approaching it). The likely result if you respond with very little by way of high cards and a dull distribution is that you will get too high. The same principle applies even more forcefully if you are playing a strong club system and 5-card majors (e.g., Precision). In that case you would still pass 1♠ on a king better than your actual hand. *Do not respond up the line when you have too few values.*

```
♠ 6              YOU      PARTNER
♡ 9 7 5          –        1♠
◇ J 10 2         ?
♣ K Q 8 7 6 5
```

Just as a simple response at the 1-level indicates at least some values (around 5-6 points), so minimum requirements apply for a 2-level response. What constitutes that minimum depends on your system, but this hand fails to qualify as a 2/1 response in any mainstream method. If you call 2♣, you will find most of opener's rebids are forcing. You will then have to bid again and take this misfit-looking hand to the 3-level.

For sure, you would like to show your clubs. Sadly your hand is not strong enough to do so. Respond 1NT. On a very good day, partner will rebid 2♣! This is not so unlikely if you are using a forcing 1NT response – with that system partner can rebid in a 3-card club suit. *Do not respond up the line when you lack the strength for a two over one response.*

```
♠ K Q 7 4        YOU      PARTNER
♡ J 9 6 5        –        1♡
◇ 6 3            ?
♣ A 10 7
```

When the deal belongs to your side the natural objective is to discover two things during the auction – firstly, which suit should be trumps and, secondly, how high you should go. Often, you must home in on the first priority early in the auction. Deciding how high to go must take a back seat until the strain is fixed. When you find your fit immediately, you can concentrate entirely on judging the level. In general, you should aim to involve partner in that decision by limiting your hand.

On a hand such as the one here, you may feel tempted to introduce your nice spade suit, but you must restrain yourself. Doing so merely confuses the issue. Tell partner which suit you want to be trumps by making a limit raise in hearts and leave the rest to him. *Do not respond up the line when supporting partner takes priority.*

	YOU	PARTNER
♠ A 3	YOU	PARTNER
♡ K Q 5 2	–	1♡
◇ A Q J 10 4	?	
♣ 9 6		

You started out with a good hand and it just turned into a giant, taking on very real slam potential. You have a number of things to tell partner – great heart fit, nice diamond suit, spade control, slam interest – and no one bid can describe them all.

As making a simple response in diamonds is likely to mean jumping to convey your strength later, you would not save any space by responding cheaply. Start with a strong jump shift to 3◇. Straight away partner also knows there may be a slam on.

Suppose partner rebids 3♡ – now you can get across the other key points of your hand with 3♠. Yes, this is a cue-bid showing a fit for hearts. Why? As we said before, you would only jump shift on a two-suited hand when partner has opened one of your suits. So, unless partner has raised you, following up with a new suit is a cue-bid agreeing opener's suit. *Do not respond up the line when you must signal slam potential.*

	YOU	PARTNER
♠ 9 6	YOU	PARTNER
♡ K 9 7	–	1♡
◇ A K J 9	?	
♣ 10 8 7 4		

Most major bidding systems use the concept of a biddable suit. This generally means that you should try to avoid bidding very poor suits such as the club suit here. You expect to raise hearts on the next round and, by calling the suit in which your values lie, you help partner to judge how well the hands mesh together. If perchance your side can make a slam, it is not very likely to be in clubs. On the other hand, if you can find 4-card diamond support opposite, you might score an extra trick with diamonds as trumps – perhaps by ruffing a club in partner's hand. A final argument in favour of the 2◇ response is that your LHO may make a pre-emptive overcall in spades. If you do end up defending, you would like to get a diamond lead. *Do not respond up the line when the suit itself is very poor.*

```
♠ Q 8 6 4        YOU        PARTNER
♡ 6 2            –          1NT
◇ J 7 5 3        ?
♣ A 8 4
```

Whether partner's 1NT shows 12-14 or 15-17 HCP, you lack the values to invite game. Despite this, perhaps you want to use Stayman in case you have a 4-4 spade fit . . .

It seems quite possible that a spade contract will play better than 1NT, but suppose partner is without four spades. Where do you want to play the hand then? Right – 1NT is the spot.

On a hand such as this, bidding over an opening 1NT offers a recipe for disaster. You *may* improve the contract if you strike lucky and find partner with four spades, but otherwise you will be lacking a paddle up the proverbial creek. ***Do not respond up the line when partner has opened 1NT and game cannot be on.***

```
♠ 10 7 5         YOU        PARTNER
♡ A J 8 3        –          1♠
◇ K Q 6          ?
♣ J 10 5
```

As we hinted a little while back, some systems (including Precision and certain of the versions of Standard American) incorporate a forcing 1NT response to a major-suit opening. That would save you from this awkward problem. So, too, would having a natural, invitational 2NT response available, but few pairs these days devote that bid to this hand type. This is rightly so, given that you usually have other ways to express a balanced 11-count – by responding in a new suit and following up with 2NT over a minimum rebid from partner.

The problem comes on this hand because you cannot bid your solitary 4-card suit, since a 2♡ response to a 1♠ opening promises at least a 5-card suit. The solution is simple enough – respond 2♣ and hope to survive. You should be able to show your invitational hand at your next turn, perhaps by raising two of a major to three. ***Do not respond up the line when you hold only four hearts in response to 1♠.***

♠ K J 10 6 5	YOU	PARTNER
♡ A Q 9 8 3	–	1♣
◇ 6 2	?	
♣ 4		

We have already seen a situation where you responded in the cheaper of two 5-card suits in the hope of finding a fit in one of them. When you are strong enough to make two bids, i.e., holding at least the values to invite game facing a minimum opening bid, you can adopt a fresh strategy that allows you to bid both suits economically.

With this hand, you should respond 1♠. If partner rebids his clubs, you can follow up with 2♡. In that case your 2♡ bid will be forcing and imply at least game invitational values, so the hand given is fairly minimum. Note that bidding up the line at your first turn does not save space this time. If you respond 1♡ initially, you would then face the prospect of rebidding 2♠ over partner's 2♣. That will force him to the 3-level if he wants to express preference for hearts. ***Do not respond up the line when you own a decent touching 5-5 hand.***

♠ 6	YOU	LHO	PARTNER	RHO
♡ Q 8 6 2	–	–	1◇	Double
◇ Q 10 7 4 3	?			
♣ J 6 5				

To which side do you think this deal belongs?

It could be yours, but the opponents seem to possess a vital advantage – they have the spade suit. If the high cards are about evenly split, they will probably outbid you.

Yes, partner might also be 4-5 in the red suits, giving you a heart fit, but so what? If the opponents have spades, they can outbid both of your suits. Your primary objective right now is to stop LHO from bidding his spade suit, and you can only hope to do that by pre-empting. Do you think bidding 1♡ will shut him out? Of course it will not. At least a jump to 3◇ stands a chance of doing so, and it also tells partner about the most important features of your hand – weak with long diamonds. ***Do not respond up the line when you need to pre-empt.***

♠ K Q 8 6	YOU	LHO	PARTNER	RHO
♡ K 9 7 4	–	1♡	2♢	Pass
♢ 10 2	?			
♣ A 9 5				

Since your LHO has bid hearts, you exclude that suit from your reckoning. This brings us to the question of whether you should mention your spades. The answer lies in what partner did not do – double 1♡ for take-out. This makes it unlikely that he has four cards in spades, the unbid major. So you should convey the overall balanced nature of your hand and your heart stopper by bidding 2NT. Partner can still introduce spades if he has something like a 4-2-6-1 shape. *Do not respond up the line when finding a fit in your suit is unlikely.*

Golden Rule Four:

Responding up the Line can

. . . Allow you to find a major-suit fit;

. . . Enable you to describe your hand;

. . . Let you show a vital feature at the one-level;

. . . Allow convenient space for finding a fit in a third suit;

. . . Offer a sensible spot when you have already passed.

Do not Respond up the Line when

. . . You have too few values;

. . . You lack the strength for a two-over-one response;

. . . Supporting partner takes priority;

. . . You must signal slam potential;

. . . The suit itself is very poor;

. . . Partner has opened 1NT and game cannot be on;

. . . You hold only four hearts in response to 1♠;

. . . You own a decent touching 5-5 hand;

. . . Finding a fit in your suit is unlikely.

Rule Five: Give Preference

Suppose you ask someone 'would you like tea or coffee' and the reply comes back 'a beer'. Does that irritate you? If so, you will relate well to this rule. When partner has shown two suits, your first duty is to consider expressing a preference between them. Sometimes you are weak and you pass, but that still amounts to giving preference. Likewise putting partner back to his first suit even though you hold more cards in his second is also showing preference, albeit false. Obeying this rule will not only keep your partner happy, but it will also get you to the right contract more often than not!

	YOU	PARTNER
♠ 7		
♡ J 9 6 5 2	–	1♠
◊ Q 8 4 3	1NT	2♣
♣ K 9 7	Pass	

Did you think about introducing your hearts at your second turn? Most likely, clubs offers only a 7-card fit, but to carry on with this misfitting collection merely invites trouble. With most systems, partner holds at least nine black cards – why should three of his remaining four cards be hearts? You want to play this type of hand as low as possible, and preferably undoubled!

	YOU	PARTNER
♠ 9 5		
♡ K 4 3	1♣	1♠
◊ A J 8	1NT	2♡
♣ A K 9 5 3	2♠	

How do you feel about bidding 2NT at your third turn? To see why doing so would be wrong, ask yourself what you have already shown with your 1NT rebid. Whether it was 15-16, or 15-17 or maybe a wide-ranging 12-16, can you claim to hold anything extra? Partner's rebid simply says that he prefers to play a suit contract rather than no-trumps. Your hand contains nothing so unusual as to suggest you might overrule him.

For sure, you may not have an 8-card fit, although partner will turn up with ten major-suit cards for this sequence most of the time. You do not know whether he is 5-5 or 6-4 in the majors, so from that point of view it looks like a guess whether to pass 2♡ or convert to 2♠. Giving false preference back to spades represents the better option, though, should partner be only 5-4. You would generally prefer a 5-2 fit to 4-3, and maybe he will bid 3♡ with 5-5. Anyway, the main point is to keep the bidding low when no guarantee of a genuine trump fit exists. *Giving preference can enable you to alight in a safe spot.*

♠ Q 8 7 5 3	YOU	PARTNER	♠ J
♡ 10 7 4 2	–	1♦	♡ Q 5 3
◇ 6 2	1♠	2♣	◇ K Q J 10 4
♣ K Q	2♦		♣ A J 8 4

When partner bids two suits, he will turn up with more cards in his first suit the majority of the time. In consequence it is rarely right to prefer his second suit with equal length.

You should therefore never pass out of fright. Your 2◇ bid does not promise 'support'. It shows 'preference'. Partner will not bid on expecting you to hold real diamond length. *Giving preference can allow for disparity of lengths.*

♠ Q 8 7 4 2	YOU	PARTNER
♡ Q 9	–	1♡
◇ 10 3	1♠	2◇
♣ A 10 6 5	2♡	

Giving preference at the lowest level also tells partner that you have no significant extra values. When you bid 2♡ here, you deny the values to do anything stronger, such as rebid 2NT or jump to 3♡. As a result, partner knows that he is facing a fairly minimum response and he will advance with caution. This conclusion applies even more strongly if you are playing 5-card majors – in that case you will typically have only a doubleton heart for this action. Either way he will need the equivalent of a 17-count to bid on. *Giving preference can limit your hand.*

	YOU	PARTNER
♠ K J 10 4 2		
♡ Q 6	–	1♡
◇ K 9 4	1♠	2◇
♣ 10 8 2	?	

Giving preference to 2♡ does not say 'I like your hearts' since with heart support you would have raised on the previous round. Apart from a desire not to stop in 2◇, it simply says 'I have nothing else to say – i.e., I have neither a decent 6-card spade suit nor the values to invite game'.

A minute ago we said that partner will know to proceed with caution when you simply give preference. Of course, that does not mean the bidding must end. Suppose his hand is:

> ♠ A Q 5
> ♡ A 9 4 3 2
> ◇ A Q J 7
> ♣ 4

In this case partner will continue with 2♠ over your simple preference to 2♡. With the same shape and a weaker hand, he would have raised your 1♠ response to the 2-level. By first introducing his diamonds, and then supporting spades even though you have shown no extra values, he indicates a significantly better hand.

> ♠ A 3
> ♡ K J 10 7 4 2
> ◇ A J 10 2
> ♣ Q

This time his hearts are strong enough to play opposite a doubleton and he has much more than he needed for an opening bid. He will therefore make a game try with a raise to 3♡, which promises a 6-card suit. With fitting honours in both of partner's suits and a hand that is clearly an above-minimum response, you will happily accept his try and go on to 4♡. ***Giving preference can keep the bidding open.***

♠ Q J 7	YOU	PARTNER
♡ K 8 6	–	1♡
◊ 4 3	2♣	2◊
♣ A J 9 6 2	?	

Preference may occur at other than the lowest available level – sometimes you can choose between partner's suits by jumping. On this hand you have enough to invite game, as well as a nice fit for partner's first suit. However, you have too little to insist on game. A jump to the 3-level in partner's first suit (3♡ here) is highly encouraging but not forcing. With any more than a bare minimum opening, partner will re-raise. *Giving preference can invite game with a jump.*

♠ A 10 9 4	YOU	PARTNER
♡ K 8 6	1NT	2◊
◊ A 5 4 2	2♡	3♣
♣ Q 8	?	

For this example we are assuming you play a weak no-trump and transfers and that 3♣ creates just a one-round force.

You have only 3-card support for partner's hearts and your high cards put you bang in the middle of the range, but your assets have grown during the auction. With the honours in partner's suits worth far more than their initial HCP value, and seemingly nothing wasted in the other two suits, it seems clear to insist on game. Jump to 4♡. *Giving preference can mean going straight to the final contract.*

♠ 7 5 2	YOU	LHO	PARTNER	RHO
♡ 8 3	–	–	1♣	1◊
◊ K 8 6 5 3	Pass	1♠	2♡	2♠
♣ Q 10 4	?			

This collection may not look very much, but with reasonable support for what must be at least a 5-card club suit, you hardly want to defend at the 2-level when the opponents have found a fit. Contest the part-score by bidding 3♣. *Giving preference can avoid your having to defend.*

♠ K Q J 9 7 4	YOU	PARTNER
♡ 6 2	–	1♡
◇ 10 7 4	1♠	2◇
♣ 6 3	?	

With partner holding at least nine red cards, the chances are that he has at most two spades, and quite likely fewer. Luckily in this case, your long suit is quite playable opposite a singleton. Moreover, your hand will contribute virtually nothing in any suit other than spades. Playing in a spade contract, you can expect to take 4-5 trump tricks in your hand plus partner's high-card winners in the other suits.

Bid 2♠. This implies no more in terms of values than your initial response did. Instead it shows a good spade suit. Partner is not invited to rebid either of his two long suits nor convert to no-trumps. Normally he will either pass or, with significant extra values, raise spades. *Do not give preference when your suit could play well facing a shortage.*

♠ K J 6	YOU	PARTNER
♡ Q 10 8 5	–	1◇
◇ K 9 4	1♡	2♣
♣ Q 10 2	2NT	

On most deals you will give preference between partner's suits with a minimum hand. Things become slightly different when you are strong enough to invite game at least. With a sound 11 HCP facing an opening bid, you want to play in game facing all but the weakest of opening bids.

One way to invite game is to jump in partner's first bid suit. Indeed, with good 3-card support, 3◇ seems reasonable on this collection. However, when your side's primary suit is a minor, you tend to aim for 3NT if looking for game.

With your balanced shape and your spade stopper(s), you should be eager to suggest a no-trump contract. Do so with 2NT rather than with 3◇. *Do not give preference when the shape and strength of your hand suggest no-trumps.*

♠ A J 9 3	YOU	PARTNER
♡ 6 4	–	1♦
♦ Q 9 6 2	1♠	2♡
♣ K 7 3	?	

As you have probably noticed, giving preference to one of partner's suits always limits your hand. Sometimes you want to give preference but cannot do so because you are too strong.

In standard methods, a 3♦ bid in the above auction would be non-forcing and consistent with a minimum response. This would be a mistake here when you know that a reverse after your 1-level response implies 16 points upwards. Of course, playing everything as forcing fails to solve the problem. You need some droppable bids when you might have only 5-7 HCP. Typically 2♠, 2NT and 3♦ are the weak, non-forcing bids.

Your choices are therefore to jump to 3NT or to force by bidding the fourth suit. Alas, neither action describes the hand well, yet you can scarcely afford to bypass 3NT merrily on this balanced shape when you may hold only a combined 26-count.

To avoid this problem, some pairs play a convention called Blackout. This uses the lower of 2NT or the fourth suit to show any poor hand (similar to Lebensohl). All other bids are then game-forcing, which allows you to bid 3♦ with this hand type.

♠ 9 6 4	YOU	PARTNER
♡ Q J 10 5	–	1♦
♦ A K 8 4	1♡	2♣
♣ A 2	?	

Problems of the nature discussed above may occur even without a reverse. In the present auction, you cannot afford to bid an invitational 3♦. Nor do you wish to bypass your most likely game (3NT) by jumping all the way to 4♦.

Establishing a forcing auction always takes precedence over showing support for partner's suit. In many cases, a bid of the fourth suit (2♠ here) provides the answer. Indeed, if partner bids either 2NT or 3♣ next, you will be able to express your diamond support with 3♦, which will then be forcing. ***Do not give preference when you must create a force first.***

	YOU	LHO	PARTNER	RHO
♠ Q 4	YOU	1♣	2♣	Double
♡ Q 2	–			
◊ Q 8 6 5 2	?			
♣ 10 7 4 3				

Here partner's cue bid promises at least 5-5 in the majors. RHO's double shows fair values and suggests an interest in defending a doubled contract. Which major should you choose?

The answer is 'neither'. You do not have a preference and RHO's double relieves you of the obligation to make a random choice. Pass and allow partner to name the suit – who knows, he may be 6-5, which would make the correct decision obvious from his side. *Do not give preference when partner is better placed to make the decision.*

Golden Rule Five:

Giving Preference can

. . . Enable you to alight in a safe spot;
. . . Allow for disparity of suit lengths;
. . . Limit your hand;
. . . Keep the bidding open;
. . . Invite game with a jump;
. . . Mean going straight to the final contract;
. . . Avoid your having to defend.

Do not Give Preference when

. . . Your suit could play well facing a shortage;
. . . The shape and strength of your hand suggest no-trumps;
. . . You must create a force first;
. . . Partner is better placed to make the decision.

Rule Six: Paint a Picture

One should regard the bidding as an opportunity to exchange information with your partner. If you succeed in expressing your hands during this period, one of you will eventually be able to 'see' both hands. Selecting the best contract then becomes relatively easy. Let us start with some examples:

	YOU	PARTNER
♠ A 4	1NT	2♡
♡ K Q 10 6	2♠	3♢
♢ K 8 4 2	?	
♣ 9 6 2		

You open a weak no-trump (12-14) and obey the transfer to spades. What should you do when partner then continues with 3♢? If you play this as only a one-round force, many contracts are still possible. They include 3♠ and 4♢, game in no-trumps, spades or diamonds, or even a slam in one of these strains. You cannot tell the best option yet. Rather than guess, the right action is to describe your hand – bid 3♡. This denies 3-card support for spades whilst telling partner you have heart values. By inference, it also suggests weak clubs as, with strength in both hearts and clubs, you would bid 3NT. *Painting a picture can show your honour location.*

	YOU	PARTNER
♠ J 6 2		1♠
♡ 10 3	–	2NT
♢ A Q 10 7 4	2♢	
♣ K 8 2	?	

Playing a weak no-trump and four-card majors, partner's 2NT rebid promises quite a strong hand (15+ and game-forcing in the modern style, but 15-16 in traditional Acol). Opposite a minimum, you still want to play in game, but which one?

Even playing 4-card majors, partner will often hold a 5-card suit. Your first priority is to uncover a potential 8-card spade fit, and you can do this by showing your 3-card support – bid 3♠.

♠ 6	YOU	PARTNER	♠ A 10 7 3 2
♡ A 10 7 3 2	1♡	1♠	♡ 5
◇ Q 4	2♣	2◇	◇ A K J 3
♣ A Q 9 6 4	?		♣ K J 2

The auction to date looks good. You have shown an opening bid with at least five hearts and four clubs. Meanwhile partner's actions indicate a decent hand with a minimum of four spades and some doubt about the final contract. He has done well – many would have jumped to 3NT upon hearing your rebid and rested there. If you now bid 3♣, you promise a 5-card club suit, which suits partner nicely. He can raise and, once you both know about the fit, it is possible to look for a slam. *Painting a picture can let you establish your combined trump length.*

♠ Q 10 8 5	YOU	PARTNER
♡ A Q 7 3	–	1♠
◇ A 8 6 5	4♣	
♣ 4		

With strong support for partner's suit, you can often explain your hand accurately with one bid. Here, a splinter jump to 4♣ achieves this. It indicates the values for at least game, 4-card or longer spade support, and at most one club. You might also make the same bid with a rather stronger hand. In that case you could continue with a cue-bid or 4NT over a 4♠ sign-off.

♠ 7	YOU	PARTNER
♡ A Q 9 6 5	1♡	2♣
◇ K 4	3♠	
♣ K J 8 6 2		

This time you are the opener, and again you have primary support for your partner's suit. Once more, a splinter bid best describes the hand. Note that one can use 3♠ to show spade shortage and club support because a 2♠ bid would be forcing. It would be inefficient to play a jump reverse as showing a 5-6 hand. If you had that, you could simply bid spades twice.

♠ 6 5	YOU	PARTNER
♡ K Q J 9 4 2	1♡	2♣
◊ A K 8	3♡	
♣ Q 6		

This hand illustrates another situation in which a bid is very expressive – the jump to 3♡ implies both extra values and a strong 6-card (or longer) suit. *Painting a picture can convey several features of your hand at once.*

♠ K 8 6	YOU	PARTNER
♡ K 6	1◊	1♠
◊ A 10 8 7 5	1NT	
♣ K Q 6		

For this example, we assume you are out of range for a 1NT opening (i.e., it would show 12-14 HCP). Now, a sound general strategy is to either open or rebid in no-trumps when holding a balanced hand. So you rebid 1NT. As a corollary to this, partner will then know that your hand is unbalanced if you open one suit and rebid in another. (An exception arises when you raise responder's suit at your second turn – generally you would not rebid in no-trumps with 4-card support for partner.) *Painting a picture can describe the overall nature of your hand.*

♠ A K 9 6 5	YOU	PARTNER
♡ Q 10 6 5 2	1♠	2◊
◊ K 4	2♡	3♣
♣ 6	?	

After partner's fourth-suit-forcing call, rebidding your hearts might look like the natural thing to do, but it wastes bidding space. A much better policy is to announce delayed diamond support by bidding 3◊. If partner continues with 3♡, showing 3-card support for that suit (or a hand too strong to sign off in 4♡), you can then let him know that you hold a fifth heart by raising to 4♡. *Painting a picture can keep the bidding low.*

♠ A 8 7 6 5 2	YOU	PARTNER
♡ A K J	1♠	2♠
◇ K 6 4	?	
♣ 3		

For this example, look to see whether you would want to end up in game facing two very similar hands for partner:

♠ K 10 4	♠ K 10 4
♡ Q 8 6	♡ Q 8 6
◇ Q J 8 2	◇ 8 7 5
♣ 8 7 5	♣ Q J 8 2

Opposite the first of these hands, where partner's diamond strength coincides with your length, game appears excellent. In contrast, when his minor-suit strength lies facing your singleton, contracting for ten tricks may well prove too ambitious.

The best way to solve this type of conundrum is for opener to bid a second suit – in this case 3◇. A suit bid in this situation neither promises a genuine (four-card) suit nor suggests that you might play the hand in anything but spades. The objective is to focus responder's attention on his holding in the second suit. In that way, he can judge how well the hands fit. ***Painting a picture can help partner know if his honours are working.***

♠ 8 6 5	YOU	PARTNER
♡ A K 7	1◇	3◇
◇ A Q J 10 5	?	
♣ 10 4		

Playing limit raises in the minor suits (rather than inverted raises), what should you rebid?

Well, where do you want to play with these two prospective hands facing you?

♠ A 10 2	♠ 9 2
♡ Q 3	♡ 8 2
◇ K 9 8 2	◇ K 8 7 3 2
♣ Q 9 8 2	♣ A K 3 2

If partner has the first hand, with stoppers in each black suit, 3NT offers the best spot. However, on the second hand, with the spades wide open, you must play in diamonds. You enlist partner's help in the decision by telling him where your strength lies – bid 3♡. This is not an attempt to play in hearts. It merely shows heart values for no-trump purposes. *Painting a picture can enable partner to judge if a no-trump contract is best.*

♠ K 9 6	YOU	PARTNER
♡ J 9	1NT	3♠
◇ K J 8 2	?	
♣ A J 10 6		

On a hand in doubt about strain, you expect partner to start with a transfer. So, except perhaps at rubber bridge, his jump to 3♠ shows two things – a good spade suit and slam interest.

If you have shown 12-14, your hand looks fairly suitable, with controls in two side suits, a fitting trump honour and a ruffing value. You could raise to 4♠ on less, so you must find some other action. The answer is to cue-bid – 4♣. This promises a club control (normally the ace) and a hand suited for slam.

♠ K 8 4 2	YOU	PARTNER	♠ A Q J 10 7 6 5
♡ A J 3	1◇	2♠	♡ 4
◇ K Q 9 4 2	?		◇ A 6
♣ 10			♣ J 7 3

Partner's jump shift says two things – it indicates at least the values for game, indeed often some slam ambition, and it also says that he has a pretty good idea what trumps are. Usually he has one of two hand types: very strong spades, as here, or both spades and diamonds. A good partner will not force on a two-suiter unless one of his suits matches yours.

You could simply raise to 3♠, but a far more descriptive bid exists – a splinter jump to 4♣. This shows both a spade fit and at most a singleton club. This is music to partner's ears. After checking on the ♡A and ♠K with Roman Key-Card Blackwood, he can jump to the excellent slam. Despite your combined 25 HCP, reaching this slam proves easy. *Painting a picture can cater for partner having ambitions beyond game.*

♠ Q 8 7	YOU	PARTNER	♠ A K J 9 2
♡ K J 10 6	–	1♠	♡ A Q 8 4
◇ J 6 5 3	2♠	3♡	◇ Q 8 2
♣ 7 2	4♡		♣ Q

Although you are playing 4-card majors, it is clear to raise spades at your first turn. When partner then makes a long-suit game try in hearts, you can suggest an alternative strain by raising. Whilst a diamond ruff might scupper either game, 4♡ will be much easier to make on a club attack.

Partner did not guarantee four hearts with his 3♡ bid but, as he does actually hold four, he has no problem passing 4♡.

♠ 6	YOU	PARTNER
♡ K 10 7 6 5 3	1♡	2◇
◇ Q	2♡	2NT
♣ A J 9 6 4	?	

You are nothing like strong enough to make a high reverse of 3♣ at your second turn – to do so would force to game and show a minimum of around 16 HCP. You therefore simply rebid your hearts. When partner advances with 2NT, you now have a chance to combine describing your hand (weak and two-suited) with suggesting an alternative to no-trumps – go 3♣. Partner can pass, raise, or correct to hearts. The one thing he should not do is to bid 3NT as he has limited his hand already. This spares you the worry about getting too high with your 10 HCP. *Painting a picture can suggest an alternative strain.*

♠ 7 4	YOU	LHO	PARTNER	RHO
♡ 10 7 4	–	–	–	1◇
◇ Q 8 2	Pass	1♠	2♡	2♠
♣ A K 8 6 3	?			

With 3-card heart support and a smattering of values, you are well worth a raise. However, simply bidding 3♡ is not the most eloquent way to make that raise. Ask yourself – if the opponents continue on to 3♠, do you really want a heart lead?

You can both show a raise in hearts to the 3-level and direct the lead by bidding 3♣. Do not worry that partner will expect just clubs – you failed to overcall either 2♣ or 3♣ at your first turn. To spring to life at this point, you must have a heart fit.

♠ 6	YOU	LHO	PARTNER	RHO
♡ K Q 9 6 5 2	1♡	1♠	2♡	4♦
◇ 6	4♡	4♠	Pass	Pass
♣ A Q 9 4 3	5♣			

Chances for lead-directing bids often come in high-level competitive auctions. As your side has bid hearts to the game level, it seems almost inconceivable that you would suddenly want to look for a new trump suit. Therefore, having elected to bid on to the 5-level, it costs nothing to tell partner where your outside strength lies in case your opponents compete further. *Painting a picture can direct the lead.*

To date we have covered a multitude of reasons for following the rule. As you have come to expect, you do not always do so:

♠ K 10 7 2	YOU	PARTNER
♡ A K J 4 3	–	Pass
◇ K 6 5	1♡	3◇
♣ 4	?	

What do you expect from partner here? He could not open the bidding, and yet now he jumps to the 3-level.

The logical explanation is that he has a sound raise to 3♡ with diamond length/values. Facing about 8-11 HCP with four hearts and five diamonds, where do you think you want to play?

Surely 4♡ is the most likely contract. You could express your hand with 3♠ on this round followed by delayed diamond support if partner calls 3NT. But why bother? This sounds like bidding for the sake of hearing the wheels go around – you have no intention of bidding a slam, nor of playing in any suit other than your 9-card major-suit fit. Describing your hand in such a situation merely serves to help the opponents to find their most effective defence. *Do not paint a picture when the description would help the defence more.*

		YOU	PARTNER
♠ 5		1♡	1♠
♡ A Q 8 6 4		2◇	2♠
◇ K J 8 3		?	
♣ A 6 5			

Bidding 3♣ or 2NT now would certainly convey your shape. Partner will know exactly the type of hand you hold. Alas, this information tells him that you are already too high! 2♠ says that he might well like to play there. To bid on with no fit you need significant extra values, which you do not hold. *Do not paint a picture when you have already bid your hand.*

		YOU	PARTNER
♠ A		–	1♡
♡ K J 10 7 5		?	
◇ K Q J 10 8 2			
♣ 4			

Here you could start with a jump-shift in diamonds, but how will this help? Surely you simply want to find out how many aces partner holds. 4NT from you should do exactly that. A 3◇ bid may bring disaster if LHO has a diamond void and doubles your heart slam, as it will be obvious which suit he wants led.

		YOU	PARTNER
♠ Q 10 7 6 5		–	1♡
♡ Q 8		1♠	2◇
◇ A K J		?	
♣ J 7 4			

Which feature of your hand do you want to show next? Nothing seems to get across all the possible options – if partner has three spades, a sixth heart or a fifth diamond, then any of those suits might prove playable. Alternatively, if he possesses a club stopper, you may belong in no-trumps.

You have no way of knowing where this auction might finish. Rather than make a descriptive bid, you would much rather ask partner to reveal more about his hand. Fortunately there is a simple way to do this – by bidding an artificial and game-forcing fourth-suit 3♣. *Do not paint a picture when it is more effective to ask than tell.*

	YOU	PARTNER
♠ A 10 9 6 2	YOU	PARTNER
♡ J 3	–	1♡
◇ A 10 4	1♠	4♡
♣ A J 5	?	

You have a number of tools on offer to investigate a slam, but none really fits the bill. If you cue-bid one minor, it sounds as if you are looking for a control in the other and you give LHO the chance to double for the lead. For sure, there is little point in wheeling out Blackwood when you hold three aces yourself. Here you really want to know whether 4♡ was a bit of a punt or whether partner was too good for a non-forcing 3♡ (and did not want to invent a non-existent minor). To test the water you advance to 5♡. With the former type of hand partner can pass and if he has the sort of hand that might have opened an Acol 2♡ if you were playing them, he can bid on. *Do not paint a picture when no single feature warrants stressing.*

	YOU	PARTNER
♠ K J 9 7 6 4	YOU	PARTNER
♡ A 2	1♠	2♣
◇ Q 8 6 4	?	
♣ 6		

On this occasion you must choose between rebidding your 6-card spade suit and introducing your diamonds. To make the decision, you need to consider what might happen on the next round of the auction. Suppose, for example, that your partner continued with 2NT. Would you not then want to show your 6-4 shape without forcing to game on your combined 21-22 HCP?

To achieve this goal, you must rebid your spades first. If partner follows with 2NT, you will have a non-forcing 3◇ bid available. If you bid 2◇ now, 3♠ over his projected 2NT rebid would be forcing. (To understand this, imagine yourself holding a stronger hand of the same shape – it could then be important to get across the 6-4 shape in order to ensure you reach the right game.) *Do not paint a picture when you lack the values to show everything.*

♠ 4 2	YOU	PARTNER
♡ Q 8	–	1♣
◇ A K 10 7 4 2	1◇	2♣
♣ A J 7	?	

This looks very awkward. We normally decry bidding suits you have not got, especially majors, but what other choice do you have? Since 3NT might be the only game you can make, you cannot afford to bypass that contract. Yet neither 2◇, 3♣ nor 3◇ would create a force. To ensure the auction continues, you must bid 2♡ (or 2♠, but at least you have Q-x of hearts).

The good news is that partner could have rebid 1♡ or 1♠ if he had a 4-card major. This makes catching an unwanted raise unlikely. Of course, that small straw hardly means you are out of the woods. Your choices on the next round may prove no more appetizing, but you can do little about that either. ***Do not paint a picture when you must set up a forcing situation.***

♠ A K Q	YOU	PARTNER
♡ Q J 6	1♣	1◇
◇ J 9 3	3NT	4♣
♣ A Q 4 3	?	

In steam-age Acol (and this is still widely played in rubber bridge clubs today), a 3NT rebid after a 1-level response shows 19 HCP. (In the same system 1NT = 15-16 and 2NT = 17-18.)

The question now arises: should you co-operate with your partner's slam try? Having already announced 19 HCP, your hand could hardly be poorer. You have only a four-card suit of your own, a poor holding in diamonds, no ruffing value, and an uncontrolled major. Do not encourage partner by supporting his diamonds or, even worse, cue-bidding your spade control. Bid 4NT, which is the most discouraging noise you can make at this point. You need not panic about this sounding like an ace ask. Common sense dictates that a 4NT bid by someone who just bid a natural, non-forcing, 3NT is almost always natural. ***Do not paint a picture when you want to apply the brakes.***

	YOU	LHO	PARTNER	RHO
♠ 6	YOU	LHO	PARTNER	RHO
♡ A Q 9 7 6 5	1♡	2◇	3♡	4◇
◇ 7 4	?			
♣ A J 8 7				

You would like to get your clubs into the auction if possible. For sure, it might help partner to decide what action to take if someone bids 5◇. Sadly, you simply cannot afford to do so – bidding 5♣ at this juncture would commit you to the 5-level anyway, and that could easily prove too high. *Do not paint a picture when the level has become too high.*

	YOU	LHO	PARTNER	RHO
♠ A K J 6 4	YOU	LHO	PARTNER	RHO
♡ 3 2	1♠	2♡	3◇	Pass
◇ 6 5	?			
♣ A Q 7 5				

Having already told partner about your spades, you would really like to show your clubs too. Alas, bidding 4♣ carries you past 3NT, which might lose your only hope of making game. Your options are to rebid your spades or to 'fudge' with a 3♡ cue bid. 3♡ carries no specific message. It simply says you have extra values but no more descriptive bid available. *Do not paint a picture when doing so may by-pass the best spot.*

	YOU	LHO	PARTNER	RHO
♠ K Q 4	YOU	LHO	PARTNER	RHO
♡ K 9 7 6 5	–	–	–	1♡
◇ A J 6	Pass	Pass	Double	Pass
♣ 7 5	Pass	2♣	2◇	Pass
	?			

As your opponents have bid two suits, you would generally cue-bid the one in which you hold a stopper. However, a little thought tells of the risk involved in a 2♡ bid. By passing the double you indicated that you expected to win seven tricks with hearts as trumps. Might not partner think you want him to leave you in 2♡? Given that you are understandably wary of jumping to 3NT with nothing in clubs, force with 3♣ instead. *Do not paint a picture when simplicity avoids a potential disaster.*

Golden Rule Six:

Painting a Picture can

. . . Show your honour location;
. . . Let you establish your combined trump length;
. . . Convey several features of your hand at once;
. . . Describe the overall nature of your hand;
. . . Keep the bidding low;
. . . Help partner know if his honours are working;
. . . Enable partner to judge if a no-trump contract is best;
. . . Cater for partner having ambitions beyond game;
. . . Suggest an alternative strain;
. . . Direct the lead.

Do not Paint a Picture when

. . . The description would help the defence more;
. . . You have already bid your hand;
. . . It is more effective to ask than to tell;
. . . No single feature warrants stressing;
. . . You lack the values to show everything;
. . . You must set up a forcing situation;
. . . You want to apply the brakes;
. . . The level has become too high;
. . . Doing so may by-pass the best spot;
. . . Simplicity avoids a potential disaster.

Rule Seven: Pace the Auction

We have focused so far on what type of message to convey. In this chapter we concentrate on the 'how'.

Most auctions contain several rounds of bidding, so you will often have a choice of which feature to show at each turn. Choosing wisely in the initial stages can smooth the later rounds of the auction and make life easier for partner, while a rash early decision may prove hard to rectify.

Unless you feel ready to place the final contract, you need to consider the rule: 'Pace the auction'.

	YOU	PARTNER
♠ K Q 9 7 6 4 2	1♠	2♡
♡ K 6 5	?	
◇ A 9		
♣ 4		

You could jump to game in either major, or maybe make a splinter bid of 4♣, but why rush to decide?

Suppose partner has one of these two hands:

♠ J 5	♠ —
♡ A Q 7 4 3	♡ A J 10 8 3 2
◇ J 4	◇ J 10 5 2
♣ Q J 6 3	♣ K Q 2

Opposite the first of these, you would rather play in spades: if hearts split 4-1, the defenders may engineer a ruff against 4♠, but that will cost them their diamond trick; the same break would almost certainly defeat 4♡. By contrast, partnering the second hand, you would surely prefer to play the heart game.

Why should you guess? Temporising with a forcing 3♠ bid may allow you to involve partner in the decision – you intend to continue with 4♡ if he rebids 3NT. He will then be well placed to make the final decision. ***Pacing the auction can involve partner in choosing the final contract.***

		YOU	PARTNER
♠	6		
♡	K Q J 8 6 4	–	1♣
◇	4	2♡	3♣
♣	A K 7 4 3		

Although it seems that all you want to know is how many aces partner has, great danger attaches to a 4NT ace enquiry. True, you could try 5♡ over a one ace (5◇) response, but you hardly want to risk playing at that level in a possible 6-1 fit. Indeed, as RKCB is often useless on minor-suit hands, some people play 4NT for another purpose, to differentiate between a sign-off and a slam try. Whilst many people play 4NT as the strong bid for ease of memory, using it as the sign-off does let you stop in 4NT. However, none of this applies if 4NT is a jump.

One solution is to employ a convention known as Kickback Blackwood, in which case 4◇ would be the ace-asking bid when clubs is the agreed suit. In reality, given that so few pairs play this, we assume you do not have that option. Therefore, we recommend a splinter-bid of 4◇ as the best action for now. Over 4♡ from partner you may continue with 4♠. If instead you hear 4♠, perhaps you will be able to make a general slam try on the next round using one of the 4NT ideas above. *Pacing the auction can avoid an embarrassing response.*

		YOU	PARTNER
♠	A 7		
♡	K 5	–	Pass
◇	A K Q 8	1♣	1♡
♣	Q J 10 9 7	?	

Facing a hand that passed as dealer you can make a pretty shrewd guess what contract you want to be in – 3NT. Even so, you should not bid no-trumps at this turn. Do you see why?

You may yet have a slam, but that is not the main reason. If partner has something like Q-x-x-(x) or K-J-x of spades, you want to have the opening lead coming up to his hand. On the other hand, opposite J-10-x, you want to protect your doubleton ace. Content yourself with a reverse bid of 2◇. Partner can then bid no-trumps with a stopper. *Pacing the auction can let you play the contract from the right side.*

```
     ♠ A 8 4           ♠ 7 3
     ♡ K Q J 10 9 4    ♡ 6
     ◇ 7 2             ◇ A Q 9 6 5
     ♣ J 3             ♣ A K 10 7 2
```

YOU	LHO	PARTNER	RHO
–	–	1◇	1♠
2♡	Pass	3♣	Pass
?			

This time it does not matter who declares a possible 3NT contract, but it would still prove a mistake to commit to that strain. Looking at both hands, it is easy to see that hearts will play significantly better than no-trumps. The defenders will knock out your spade ace at trick one and, with it, your entry to five heart winners. On this occasion, you can foresee the hitch without needing to catch sight of partner's hand. Forget about 3NT and rebid your semi-solid heart suit – call 3♡. *Pacing the auction can mean projecting how the play is likely to go.*

```
     ♠ 7 4        YOU   PARTNER   ♠ A K 9 6 5
     ♡ K J 6      –     1♠        ♡ Q 10 8 7 4
     ◇ A Q 9 6 4  2◇    2♡        ◇ J 3
     ♣ K 7 3      ?               ♣ 2
```

More often than not you will wind up in 3NT, but stabbing at it now could backfire badly. Facing partner's actual hand, surely you would rather play in 4♡ than 3NT?

Perhaps you believe that partner should continue with 4♡ if you jump to 3NT, but this would be quite wrong. Leaps to game send a clear message – 'this is the right spot unless you have something really unexpected.' Partner would need to be 6-5 in the majors before he should even consider bidding again.

A jump to 3NT should show little interest in other contracts. On this hand, mark time with an artificial fourth-suit-forcing bid of 3♣. If partner cannot rebid his hearts, you will be able to bid 3NT at your next turn. This route to 3NT (going via fourth-suit) expresses doubt about the final contract. *Pacing the auction can leave partner room to describe his hand.*

	YOU	PARTNER
♠ J 2	YOU	PARTNER
♡ 6 4	–	1 ♡
◇ K Q 10 7 6 3	2 ◇	2 ♠
♣ K J 5	?	

Your attractive six-card diamond suit certainly warrants a rebid, but does this look like the right moment?

Partner's reverse bid after your 2-level response has created a game-forcing auction, so you can bid anything you like below game without fearing an abrupt end to the auction. There are two features of your hand to get over – your long diamonds and your club stopper. Which takes precedence?

To see why you should choose to show your club guard first (by bidding 2NT now), put yourself in partner's shoes for a moment. Suppose you bid 3 ◇ in the auction given – what is he supposed to do next with a 4-5-2-2 shape that includes two low clubs? He cannot rebid either of his majors without giving a false picture of his shape, and he can hardly bid 3NT with no cover in the fourth suit. He may therefore be forced into raising diamonds, thus bypassing what may be the only making game.

See how much better things work out if you bid 2NT. Partner can support your diamonds (with a 4-5-3-1 shape) or probe via a fourth-suit 3 ♣ bid if he is unsure about the final contract. With nothing more than he has already promised, he can also raise to 3NT without worrying about clubs. *Pacing the auction can forestall partner's problems.*

	YOU	LHO	PARTNER	RHO
♠ 7 4	YOU	LHO	PARTNER	RHO
♡ K J 9 6	1 ◇	2 ♠	3 ♣	Pass
◇ A K Q 9 7 2	?			
♣ 6				

A cue bid of 3 ♠ here would suggest that you do not have a clearcut descriptive bid to make. Making such a call on this hand would be an error – it simply delays the problem until the next round of the auction. If partner bids 3NT over your cue-bid, will you feel happy about passing?

You must choose between a simple rebid in diamonds and introducing your hearts. If you rebid 3♡, you will have to guess at your next turn – should you pass 3NT or show your strong diamonds? The answer is to make the cheapest call now – 3♢. With four hearts, partner can bid them. If he says 3NT, you can pass, knowing that you have shown your diamonds and catered for a potential 4-4 heart fit as well. You need not worry about him passing 3♢ – if he does, he probably has something like a 3-3-1-6 10-count, so you will not be missing anything. *Pacing the auction can spare you a problem at your next turn.*

♠ A	YOU	PARTNER
♡ J 4	1♢	1♡
♢ K Q 10 7 6 4 2	3♢	4♣
♣ K Q 7	?	

As 4♣ must be an advance cue-bid agreeing diamonds, it seems natural to bid 4♠ now. However, that prevents partner from cue-bidding hearts at the four-level. True, he might go 5♡, but then you waste a whole round of bidding. It is much better to temporise with 4♢ and leave him room to continue with 4♡. *Pacing the auction can allow partner room to cue-bid.*

♠ 7	YOU	PARTNER	♠ A K Q 8 6
♡ A K 9 6 2	–	1♠	♡ 8 4
♢ K 10 2	2♡	3♢	♢ A Q J 9 4
♣ J 10 9 4	3NT	4♢	♣ 3
	?		

You cannot tell whether partner is simply seeking the best game or whether he is interested in a slam, but it matters not. Rather than lazily putting him up to 5♢, bid 4♡ *en route* – this must be a cue-bid as you would have bid 3♡ rather than 3NT at your previous turn if you simply had a long string of hearts. If you fail to do so, partner may well assume that you hold neither missing ace and stop in game. You need not worry about sounding too strong as you made a non-forcing 3NT bid at your second turn. *Pacing the auction can cater for partner having slam interest.*

	YOU	PARTNER
♠ A 2		
♡ K J 8 7 6	1♡	3◇
◇ J 5	?	
♣ K Q 7 4		

Are you thinking of introducing your club suit?

If so, ask yourself why. Can clubs ever become trumps after this start to the auction? No – when partner makes a jump shift, he should already know which suit will be trumps. Jump shifts should normally be used on only two types of hand: excellent diamonds and at least some slam interest, or primary (4-card) heart support and a good diamond suit on the side. If he has the first type of hand, you will end up playing in diamonds (or no-trumps). With the second, hearts will clearly be trumps.

The best move when partner makes a jump shift is to leave him the maximum amount of room to tell you why he jumped. Bidding 3♡ here achieves that objective – partner can continue with either 3NT or 4◇ (to show the single-suited type of hand) or with anything else to agree hearts. *Pacing the auction can allow partner to clarify his intentions.*

	YOU	PARTNER
♠ A 9 3		
♡ A K 2	–	Pass
◇ A Q 6	?	
♣ A K Q 7		

What do you see here? You have a balanced hand, all suits stopped, plenty of potential winners and enough high cards to warrant game. Yet of course you cannot open 3NT. If you do that, partner will place you with a quite different type of hand – a solid minor and little outside. He might then pass when you can make a slam or, just as bad, remove you from what could be your last making contract because he thinks his hand is too weak. *Pacing the auction can avoid showing a wrong specific hand type.*

It usually pays not to rush things. Even so, you will come across hands on which a direct bash provides the answer. Our next example provides a case in point.

		YOU	PARTNER
♠	7	YOU	PARTNER
♡	K 9 6 4 2	–	1 ♡
◊	K J 10 9 2	?	
♣	J 4		

Do you feel tempted to respond 2◊?

For sure, you plan to support hearts vigorously next time, and the knowledge of your diamond length may help partner to judge how well the hands fit. This could help him make the correct decision about trying for a slam or, should the enemy come in, whether or not to bid one more. However, two sharp downsides attach to this circuitous method of showing heart support. For one, a delayed game raise suggests rather more by way of high cards than this hand contains. For another, a response at the lowest level gives your LHO an easy chance to enter the auction. So jump to 4♡. *Do not pace the auction when you want to pre-empt the opposition.*

		YOU	LHO	PARTNER	RHO
♠	A K J 10 7 6 5	YOU	LHO	PARTNER	RHO
♡	K Q J 10	–	–	–	1 ◊
◊	K	Double	Pass	2 ♣	Pass
♣	Q	?			

This is a powerful collection – your seven-card major should yield six or seven tricks and, after drawing trumps, you can knock out the ace of hearts for three more tricks. That said, a delicate auction starting with a 2◊ cue-bid would be misguided. Facing a hand that could only muster a minimum response to your initial double, prospects for slam are non-existent. So why risk partner thinking that you cherish higher ambitions or that you do not know which strain to play in? You have no need to do anything special at this point to say you hold a strong hand. The very fact you started with a take-out double rather than some sort of overcall achieved that. Take all the pressure off him by jumping to 4♠. *Do not pace the auction when you already know what the best spot should be.*

The theme of curtailing the auction to deny interest in higher things recurs on our next hand.

♠ 7 2	YOU	PARTNER	♠ A K J 10 4 3
♡ K 9 7 3	–	1♠	♡ A Q 6 2
◇ K Q 10 4	2◇	2♡	◇ 7 2
♣ K Q 7	?		♣ 4

Whilst you cannot afford to make a non-forcing bid, a clear danger exists that if you pussyfoot around with a fourth-suit 3♣, partner may think you are not sure which suit should be trumps. Suppose he then bids 3♠ and you convert to 4♡. Could this be a cue-bid agreeing spades? Alternatively, partner may expect a much stronger heart raise from you and advance towards slam.

If hearts break 4-1, you might pay a heavy price for any foray to the 5-level and the blame will fall entirely on your side of the table. As we said earlier, you take things slowly to express doubt. The implication of this is that you must arrive at your destination quickly if you know where you are going. The same applies even if you are playing two-over-one game force and could bid a forcing 3♡. Just put him to 4♡ and get yourself ready to display the dummy. ***Do not pace the auction when you should be using fast arrival.***

♠ J 6	YOU	PARTNER
♡ A J 7	1♣	1♠
◇ K 2	3NT	
♣ A K J 10 7 4		

As we said in chapter 6, using a 3NT double jump rebid to convey a balanced 19 count is an inefficient use of the bid. It seldom crops up and, in any event, partner may want room to investigate other contracts, which he will not have after this giant leap.

By using a 1NT opening and a 1NT rebid to cater for flat hands in the 12-14 and 15-17 ranges respectively (vice versa in a strong no-trump structure), a 2NT jump rebid shows 18-19. This releases the gargantuan jump to 3NT for another purpose – namely to show a hand well suited to the no-trump game, usually with stoppers in the unbid suits, but essentially based on a source of tricks.

Such a treatment seems ideal for your present hand. It saves you from juggling with the underbids of 3♣ and 2NT, or maybe inventing a 2♡ reverse. The fact that you get across the precise nature of your hand amply justifies gobbling up so much bidding space. ***Do not pace the auction when a single bid describes your hand well.***

Golden Rule Seven:

Pacing the Auction can

. . . Involve partner in choosing the final contract;
. . . Avoid an embarrassing response;
. . . Let you play the contract from the right side;
. . . Mean projecting how the play is likely to go;
. . . Leave partner room to describe his hand;
. . . Forestall partner's problems;
. . . Spare you from a problem at your next turn;
. . . Allow partner room to cue-bid;
. . . Cater for partner having slam interest;
. . . Allow partner to clarify his intentions;
. . . Avoid showing a wrong specific hand type.

Do not Pace the Auction when

. . . You want to pre-empt the opposition;
. . . You already know what the best spot should be;
. . . You should be using fast arrival;
. . . A single bid describes your hand well.

Rule Eight: Bid Your Games

Should you push hard to bid game?

The answer to that question depends on the scoring method and, sometimes, the vulnerability. At match-points (normal pairs) or point-a-board (also known as board-a-match) scoring, you strive to outscore other pairs holding your cards, but the margin by which you do so carries little relevance. In these types of competition, you can reap handsome rewards simply by going plus on most boards. Therefore, you should avoid stretching to a game that might fail more often than it makes.

Playing rubber bridge, IMPs (teams) and Chicago a different situation exists. You might think you should exercise particular caution when your side is vulnerable, but in truth the exact opposite applies. If you watch top players in action, you will notice that they bid vulnerable games very aggressively. To understand why, bear with us while we run through some simple arithmetic.

In a teams match, suppose the two North–South pairs are dealt consecutive potential major-suit game hands. In each case, one pair bids game and the other stops in a part-score.

Suppose on the first of these deals N–S is non-vulnerable. If nine tricks represent the limit of the hand, the team whose N–S pair stopped in a partial will get +140 at one table and +50 at the other – a 5-IMP gain. However, when the defenders' cards sit favourably and ten tricks roll in, the team bidding on will record +420 and -170 – a swing of 6 IMPs.

Assuming that you could always guarantee coming within one trick of your contract and nobody ever doubled, you would break even by consistently bidding non-vulnerable games when the odds were 5:6 against making. To cater for the occasional time when you go more than one down or someone doubles, you will not go far wrong if you assume that you want to bid non-vulnerable games requiring no more than a finesse.

Surprisingly, perhaps, you can afford much poorer odds when vulnerable . . .

In the same scenario, when nine tricks are available, the team stopping in the part-score will go plus in both rooms (+140 and +100) for a 6-IMP pick-up. On the other hand, when ten tricks make, the team bidding on will score +620 and -170 for a 10-IMP gain. Subject to the same criteria discussed above, you want to have a shot at a vulnerable game at IMPs whenever the odds are better than 6:10 against. As a rough rule of thumb, you want to reach a vulnerable game that at worst depends on a 3-3 break, or one that requires a 3-2 break and a finesse. Finally, remember that many players find defence really tough and plenty of dodgy contracts make it through the slips.

♠ A J 8 6 5	YOU	PARTNER
♡ A 7 4 3	–	1♢
♢ 6 5	1♠	2♠
♣ J 4	?	

4♠ can be 50% at best and you cannot say that the 3-level looks totally safe. At match-points and similar types of scoring, you should pass and ensure your plus. By contrast, vulnerable at IMPs, you should invite game with 3♡. *Bidding your games can let you score a lucrative game bonus.*

♠ K Q 9 7 4	YOU	PARTNER	♠ J 10 6 3	
♡ A K J 2	1♠	2♠	♡ Q 4	
♢ A	4♠		♢ K J 9 4	
♣ Q 6 4			♣ 9 5 2	

Seeing only your two hands, it looks as if you want to stay out of the inevitable 4♠. You count one sure trump loser and likely three in clubs. However, when you think how the defence might proceed, the picture becomes rather different. People rarely underlead aces and many shy away from king-high suits.

A passive red-suit opening will enable you to discard a club on the king of diamonds before drawing trumps. Even if North has a holding such as ♣A-K-J-x, and hence an automatic club lead, it may not be so easy for him to find the trump switch needed to get South in for a club return. *Bidding your games can allow you to capitalise on a favourable opening lead.*

	YOU	PARTNER
♠ 8 6		2♣
♡ 9 7 4 3	–	
◇ 6 5 4 2	2◇	2♠
♣ 10 8 4	2NT	3♡
	?	

With this dismal collection you may feel inclined to pass now that partner has called a suit you quite like, but doing so would constitute an error. In most systems partner's 2♣ indicates that he can almost see game in his own hand. This makes you duty bound to keep the bidding open one more round. Remember, you have yet to promise any values, which means that a simple raise to 4♡ in no way overstates them. Indeed, if you play 2◇ as a denial and 2NT as a second negative, he already knows you hold next to nothing. This should make him pretty pleased to find four-card support for one of his suits. *Bidding your games enables you to honour a forcing sequence.*

Keeping your partner happy gave a good reason to press on with that last hand, and a similar theme occurs here:

	YOU	PARTNER
♠ A K 8 6 5	1♠	2♡
♡ 9 7 4 3	?	
◇ K J 10		
♣ 4		

With this 11-count one's instincts may suggest a minimum rebid, but again the hand warrants a closer look. If you raise to 3♡ and partner thinks for a while before passing, how will you feel? Worried, we suspect. Whilst you have no HCP to spare, you should value the shape highly. The 2♡ response promised at least a five-card suit, which gives you nine or more trumps between you. Moreover your hand offers two ways to contribute a fair few tricks as dummy, both via long spades and club ruffs.

An extra problem may arise if you huddle before giving a single raise. On any remotely marginal hand partner may feel barred from going on. True, raising on a very strong doubleton provides an alternative explanation for a slow 3♡, but directors (and appeals committees) rarely see things that way. *Bidding your games can take the pressure off partner.*

Tactical considerations come to the fore on our next case, too. This time your opponents have not given you a free run:

♠ K Q 8 7 6 4 2	YOU	LHO	PARTNER	RHO
♡ 6	1♠	2♡	2♠	3♡
◇ A 8 4	?			
♣ Q 6				

Jumping to game here represents a two-way shot. Okay, you will need to catch partner with just the right hand if you are to make ten tricks, but do you ever intend to defend 4♡?

Of course you will compete further, but if you pass or bid 3♠ now and then call 4♠ when LHO's 4♡ bid comes back to you, it will become clear to the opponents that you are sacrificing. Two good things can happen by bidding game straight away. For one, the opponents may allow you to play undoubled when they can make game and 4♠ is going one or two down. For another, they may misjudge and bid on to the 5-level as a save, thinking that your side owns the hand and can make game. *Bidding your games can cause the opponents to misjudge.*

♠ J 10 6 5	YOU	PARTNER
♡ K 10 4	–	1NT
◇ Q 10 3	?	
♣ A 6 2		

The bonus of 100 points for a part-score not converted into game if a rubber ends incomplete is also a fair reflection of its value in a normal rubber. This means that if the opponents have a part-score, game your way assumes greater value than usual, up to 600 (500 plus 100) with both sides vulnerable. If you are non-vulnerable (which will be the case here if you are playing a variable no-trump) game is worth around 450 points (350 plus 100) but the penalty for going off remains at 50 per trick. So, facing a 12-14 1NT and despite your sterile shape, you might consider putting partner up to 2NT. If he then bids and makes 3NT, you will both clock up your own game and nullify their part-score. *Bidding your games can wipe out an opposing part-score at rubber bridge (or Chicago).*

♠ K 9 6	YOU	PARTNER
♡ 7 4	1◊	1♠
◊ A Q 9 6 5	2♠	3♣
♣ Q J 7	?	

Vulnerable at IMPs, would you feel very tempted to accept partner's game try?

You should not be. Partner also knows the form of scoring and yet could only invite game. If he wanted to play in 4♠ opposite a lousy minimum, an apt description for this hand, he would have bid it himself. Indeed, it should scarcely surprise you to find that the 3-level is one too high. ***Not bidding your games can be right when you have already bid to the limit.***

♠ K J 6	YOU	LHO	PARTNER	RHO
♡ A K 8 7 5	1♡	1♠	2♡	Pass
◊ K 4	?			
♣ Q 10 4				

Although you have 16 HCP and partner might turn up with as many as nine, LHO's spade overcall suggests your honours may not pull their full weight. Moreover, RHO's failure to raise spade hints at shortness there, which increases the likelihood that he holds length in the other three suits, including hearts.

As game rates to be marginal at best, you should pass now. Often eight tricks will prove the limit of the deal.

♠ K J 5	YOU	LHO	PARTNER	RHO
♡ 10 7 4 3	–	Pass	1♡	2◊
◊ 8 4 3	2♡	Pass	2♠	Pass
♣ K 7 6	?			

True, you have some help in spades and a fourth trump to boot, but oh, what an awful lot of losers. Also, three low is the worst possible diamond holding. As the suit has only been bid once, partner rates to turn up with two or three diamonds. Any honour he has there is likely to be worthless and your dummy hardly provides a great source of discards. ***Not bidding your games can save you when the cards figure to lie badly.***

♠ Q 7	YOU	PARTNER
♡ A Q J 9 6	1♡	2♡
◊ K 10 3 2	?	
♣ A J		

Whilst you have 17 HCP and a good suit, ten tricks seem some way off. For example, give partner any hand with the ♡K, no black-suit singleton and either three or four diamonds to the ace, and you probably have four inescapable losers. For game to be good facing a minimum raise, you probably need partner to produce short diamonds and some black-suit help, and you cannot sensibly find out about that.

Even opposite the wrong maximum, game may still have no chance. Nonetheless, if you were told that partner held nine points rather than six, you would want to go for game. So make a try and respect partner's decision. ***Not bidding your games can mean making a try instead.***

♠ A 10 8 6	YOU	PARTNER
♡ A Q 10 2	1♣	1◊
◊ 5	1♡	1NT
♣ K Q 7 5	2♠	3♠
	?	

Playing match-point pairs you need to answer yourself two questions at this point. Firstly, is 3♠ forcing? Secondly, if not, should you bid one more all the same?

Given partner's limit 1NT bid you cannot regard 3♠ as in any way forcing. Indeed he may have raised simply because he thought he could not pass. The key here is that many pairs will fail to get into the fourth suit, so why risk a good score? There is another reason to tread warily. With 8 HCP, five diamonds and four decent spades you would expect partner to respond 1♠ rather than 1◊. His actual choice suggests bad spades.

At the table, the player who held this hand did advance to 4♠. With some help from the defence, he proceeded to make 11 tricks and record a 97% score. However, +200 would have yielded 78%. ***Not bidding your games can work fine if simply making the tricks will score well.***

	YOU	PARTNER
♠ 6		
♡ K J 8 6 5 2	1♡	1♠
◇ K Q 4	2♡	2♠
♣ A J 7	?	

Partner's 2♠ bid is scarcely encouraging, although he should not be too weak as your rebid showed a decent 6-card suit yourself and he could have passed 2♡ with a really bad hand. You can expect him to hold somewhere in the region of 8-10 points, a 6-card spade suit, and short hearts. This means your side might own as many as 24 HCP. Even so, proceeding further on this 'misfit' would represent an unwise policy.

	YOU	PARTNER
♠ K J 9 6 5		
♡ 6	–	1♡
◇ Q 4	1♠	2◇
♣ A Q 9 6 2	?	

You were probably brought up to believe that an opening bid facing an opening bid will generally produce game. This is a sound philosophy and you should normally try for a game in those circumstances. That said, the trend towards ever weaker opening bids means exceptions are less rare than they were.

Indeed there are times to break almost every rule, golden or otherwise. This hand illustrates the type of occasion on which you should feel prepared to stop short of game despite holding a full opening bid opposite partner's opener. Partner holds at least nine red cards. In which suit do you propose to play? If you are thinking of 3NT, picture a minimum hand opposite with 5-5 in the red suits and then ask yourself where you will find nine tricks. An invitational 2NT is quite enough on this hand.

We will cover how to treat misfit hands in more detail with chapter 10. For now, suffice it to say that you exercise caution when it becomes clear that your side has no fit. *Not bidding your games can prove sensible when the hands fit poorly.*

On this example you had to listen attentively to partner's bidding to work out that your hands might not mesh together well. With the case at the top of the next page, you can tell largely from your own hand whether to brake or accelerate.

♠ A K 7 3 2
♥ J 6 5
♦ Q 8 3
♣ A 5

Imagine that partner deals and opens 1♠ on this collection. Now consider these three possible hands for you:

♠ 10 8 6 4	♠ 10 8 6 4	♠ 10 8 6 4
♥ Q 9 4 3 2	♥ K Q 9 4 2	♥ K Q 9 4 2
♦ K	♦ K	♦ 4
♣ K 10 3	♣ 10 4 3	♣ K 10 3

Each responding hand has the same shape and number of high cards, yet you might choose three different responses. What is more, you would be justified in doing so.

The count of high-card points and distributional points can only provide a rough guide. The true value of your honours will depend upon how well they do the job of creating tricks. In general, honours in combination (either with those in your hand or in partner's), particularly if they are in long suits, will tend to pull the full weight. On the other hand, unsupported honours, especially ones in short suits, may prove worthless.

Clearly, the weakest of the three hands shown above is the first, where the diamond king may be waste paper. You can count however many points you like for the singleton, but you cannot also add another three for that king because it is bare. The heart and club honours may all come in handy, although one would hardly want to bet on it. If you use the 'Losing Trick Count', you will view this as a 9-loser hand, which suggests a raise to 2♠. Indeed that sounds like a suitable valuation to us.

The second hand is better, since the side-suit honours take on a much higher value now they support each other. A limit raise to 3♠ feels about right with this assortment.

The third hand offers still more potential. We do not advise a 2♥ response as returning to spades later would then suggest a rather better hand, but we would want to go for game. Jump to 4♠ with this 7-loser hand. *Not bidding your games can turn out well if your honours lie in short suits.*

	YOU	LHO	PARTNER	RHO
♠ K J 4				
♡ J 9 6	–	–	1♡	2♢
♢ 6 4	2♡	3♢	Double	Pass
♣ K 7 4 3 2	?			

LHO's raise has used up all of the space normally available for partner to make a trial bid, which creates a problem. The answer is to use double in this auction as a game try and 3♡ as purely competitive. So, should you accept the invitation?

Yours looks like a middle-of-the-road raise to 2♡ – neither maximum nor minimum. Are there any other clues?

Yes – the opponents' bidding suggests that they will hold nine diamonds, which places partner with a doubleton. This means your ruffing value will add nothing in the play. As a general principle, the worst possible length in the enemy suit is three cards when only one opponent has bid the suit and two when they have bid and raised. This should tip the balance in favour of conservatism here. *Not bidding your games can be prudent when you both have the same shortage.*

	YOU	LHO	PARTNER	RHO
♠ K 10 7 6 5				
♡ J	–	–	1♡	2♣
♢ A Q 6	2♠	Pass	3♠	Pass
♣ 9 7 5 2				

Looking at a fairly minimum 2♠ bid, you hear partner issue a single raise. Should you throw caution to the wind?

Your shape rather than the count of your high cards should lead you to the correct answer. For a start, the singleton in partner's first-bid suit hardly constitutes an asset. Also, you have four losers in RHO's suit. Any club honours partner holds lie under the bidder and are, therefore, of dubious value. In addition, LHO is almost certain to lead a club through partner's holding at trick one. Added to all that, partner rates to have only three trumps for his single raise, so how will you ruff all of your club losers even if you find partner relatively short in the suit? Just pass. *Not bidding your games can win when you hold length in the wrong place.*

Golden Rule Eight:

Bidding Your Games can

   . . . Let you score a lucrative game bonus;
   . . . Allow you to capitalise on a favourable opening lead;
   . . . Enable you to honour a forcing sequence;
   . . . Take the pressure off partner;
   . . . Cause the opponents to misjudge;
   . . . Wipe out an opposing part-score at rubber (or Chicago).

Not Bidding Your Games can

   . . . Be right when you have already bid to the limit;
   . . . Save you when the cards figure to lie badly;
   . . . Mean making a game try instead;
   . . . Work fine if simply making the tricks will score well;
   . . . Prove sensible when the hands fit poorly;
   . . . Turn out well if your honours lie in short suits;
   . . . Be prudent when you both have the same shortage;
   . . . Win when you hold length in the wrong place.

Rule Nine: Be Conservative in the Slam Zone

Bidding and making a slam is exciting, yet the fact remains that many pairs would be better off if they never sought such dizzy heights. At lower levels, one can rely on general values and some sort of fit to guide you. In the slam zone more precision is required. To take twelve or thirteen tricks you must first have the assets to gather that many winners. You also need the requisite control cards to stop the enemy beating you quickly, and the trump suit, if there is one, must be robust.

Once again, we begin with some arithmetic. Suppose you reckon you can make eleven or twelve tricks with spades as trumps and that you are unlikely to get doubled if you misjudge.

At most forms of scoring you stand to gain almost exactly as much as you might lose if you proceed to a slam. When you are not vulnerable, you could gain 500 (the small slam bonus) by bidding on or lose the same amount (the 450 you would have made plus the 50 lost for going one down). Vulnerable the figures become 750 in each case (5♠ making is now 650 and 6♠-1 costs 100).

It sounds like you want to be in a small slam on a 50% shot, i.e., a simple finesse. In practice, though, the field (or the other room, as the case may be) might reach contracts other than game or slam in the right suit. It has been known for people to play eleven or twelve trick hands in a part-score, or a grand slam, or the wrong suit, or perhaps defend with them. All these factors combined mean that you effectively need better than 50-50 odds to warrant going for the slam bonus.

The only real difference comes at rubber bridge where you have no other results to bring in to the equation. Even then the odds are normally the same as at teams scoring – although at times a desire to win the rubber quickly or by a wide margin might influence you one way or the other. The strength of the potential declarer can also swing the decision. Martin Hoffman could tell you that his partners are forever putting him in to thin slams because they know he handles the dummy so well.

♠ A Q 10	YOU	PARTNER	♠ J 9 6
♡ K Q 5	2NT	4NT	♡ J 10 8
◇ A Q 7 4	?		◇ K 8 6 3
♣ K J 7			♣ A Q 9

In terms of high cards, you have a pretty average 2NT opening bid – neither minimum nor maximum if you play the range as 20-22 HCP. Having said that, hands with a 4-3-3-3 pattern frequently fail to generate as many tricks as their point count might suggest. Either a fifth diamond or a second 4-card suit would increase the prospective playing strength of the hand. Unfortunately, with your actual 4-3-3-3 shape, you are likely to run out of winners before time.

And so it proves – slam on these cards not only needs the spade finesse to work, but diamonds to break 3-2 as well. That makes it roughly a 34% shot. Bidding a slam can gain you 11 or 13 IMPs (depending on the vulnerability) one time in three and lose a similar amount almost exactly twice as often. At pairs the odds are the same. Either way you will do well in the long run to stay out of a slam on this type of deal. *Being conservative in the slam zone can protect your game bonus.*

The advice to exercise caution applies more strongly when contemplating a grand slam. Apart from missing the chance of an easy game (and perhaps wrapping up a rubber) you are also putting the small slam bonus at risk. If, instead of settling for a safe 6♠, you push on to 7♠, you hope to gain an extra 500 points non-vulnerable or 750 vulnerable. At total points, you risk losing 1030 (980 plus 50) and 1530 (1430 plus 100) respectively. This implies you need round about a two-thirds chance to justify trying for the grand slam. However, peripheral factors again mean you really want to play it safer than that. Others may stop in game, or play in the wrong suit or suffer some other type of mix-up. It is quite amazing how often one scores +680 for missing a slam and find yourselves gaining 13 IMPs because your opponents at the other table went down in a grand slam. This can happen even at International level. For example, in the England v Wales match in the 2001 Camrose, one side had a misunderstanding and stopped in game whilst the other bid a grand slam missing queen to four trumps.

♠ A K 8 6 5	YOU	PARTNER	♠ Q 4 2
♡ –	1♠	2♣	♡ 10 7 6 3
◇ K J 10 7 3	2◇	3♠	◇ A Q 2
♣ A Q 4	6♠		♣ K 10 3

You could consider yourself very unlucky if you were unable to make twelve tricks in either spades or diamonds, and a grand slam requires little more than a 3-2 spade break. Even allowing for the slight chance of a 5-0 diamond break, the grand slam is about a 2:1 favourite.

Here, with just 28 HCP between the two hands and only an 8-card fit, a very real chance exists that others may not get past game. Playing pairs in a large field, you could expect to get about 75-80% for bidding a small slam in spades. Bidding and making the grand will increase that to around 95%, whilst going down in seven will score virtually nothing. *Being conservative in the slam zone can protect your small slam bonus.*

♠ A K Q 2	YOU	PARTNER	♠ 9 4
♡ K Q 7 6 5	1♡	3♣	♡ A 4 2
◇ 8 6	3♡	4♡	◇ Q 9
♣ J 7	?		♣ A K Q 10 8 4

With 15 HCP, a fair suit, a fitting honour for partner's suit, and such good spade controls, are you tempted to bid on?

One can easily to see what might happen if you do so. You will discover that you are missing a diamond control and stop at the 5-level, but do you think you will manage to alight in the relatively safe 5♣? More likely you are going to get to 5♡. If the trumps then misbehave, you will find yourself going minus. Partner's failure to make an advance cue-bid sounds a loud warning, which you should heed. *Being conservative in the slam zone can save you from going down in a slam try.*

Accurate bidding of minor-suit slams presents a particular problem at match-point pairs. Once you have bypassed the high-scoring 3NT, you may feel compelled to proceed on to a slam because +400 or +420 in 5♣/5◇ will score almost as poorly as -50 if the room is +430 or +460. You may get around this by signing off in 4NT, but not always.

♠ K J 7	YOU	PARTNER	♠ Q 2
♡ A K 6	1◊	3◊	♡ 7 4
◊ K Q 8 7 6	?		◊ A J 9 4
♣ K 4			♣ Q J 10 6 2

Having not opened 2NT, you could hardly be much better and partner certainly might produce the right hand to give a diamond slam good play. However, to find out whether he has both two aces and the necessary major-suit shortages (or queens), you will need to commit to game in diamonds rather than no-trumps. Playing match-points, to do so would be a losing tactic – for every occasion you reach a good slam, you will find many when you score very poorly for +400 while the field is making overtricks in 3NT. *Being conservative in the slam zone can avoid a low-scoring game at pairs.*

If you are playing rubber bridge (or Chicago) and the enemy has a part-score then game your way is worth more than usual. In addition to its inherent value, a game score will deny your opponents the chance to convert their partial into a game. *Being conservative in the slam zone can let you zap an opposing part-score at rubber bridge or Chicago.*

The converse of this rubber bridge application of the rule applies when your side has the part-score: if you bid a failing slam, all is not lost. Except on the final deal of the session (or the stanza playing Chicago), your side will retain its part-score and thus remain favourite to notch up the next game.

So, in this situation you can be freer than usual in your slam bidding. An added quirk at Chicago only arises if you are not vulnerable on the current hand. In this instance your retained part-score (if you contract for a failing slam) might help you to obtain a vulnerable game bonus later. *Being aggressive in the slam zone can be okay if you have a part-score at rubber bridge or Chicago.*

Those last two paragraphs notwithstanding, do you get the impression from the early part of this chapter that you should give up slam bidding altogether? We would like to rectify that now, as accurate slam bidding can generate many IMPs and match-points. It also separates the regular winners from the rest in many rubber bridge clubs.

♠ Q 6 4	YOU	PARTNER	♠ A K
♡ A 7	–	1♣	♡ K J 8
◇ K Q 9 7 6 4 3	1◇	2NT	◇ A 5 2
♣ A	3◇	4◇	♣ K 9 7 6 5
	4♡	4♠	
	4NT	5♡	
	5NT	7◇	

Your hand keeps improving as the auction develops. When partner rebid 2NT you sensed a probable slam. Now he freely supports your strong 7-card suit, you can go off to the races.

It is generally wrong to launch into Blackwood when you have a suit with two top losers (spades here). Whilst it seems unlikely partner would call 2NT with a jack-high spades, it costs nothing to find out. By cue-bidding in hearts first, you make it easy for him to show a spade control – then you can bid 4NT.

Partner confirms both missing aces with his 5♡ response and your ensuing 5NT states interest in a grand slam. With a third trump and all his values working, he jumps to the 7-level.

♠ A Q 10 8 3	YOU	PARTNER	♠ K 7 5 4
♡ 6	1♠	3♠	♡ K J 7 2
◇ Q 2	4♣	4◇	◇ A 3
♣ A K Q J 5	4NT	5♡	♣ 8 6 2
	6♠		

When partner makes a limit raise in spades, you know your excellent club suit will provide a source of tricks. Making a slam therefore hinges on whether the enemy can take the first two tricks. Here, too, you must cue-bid before using Blackwood.

The first move is to ensure that you do not have two top diamond losers, and you can do this by cue-bidding in clubs. If partner cannot make a suitable return cue-bid, you will happily settle for game knowing that no slam is available.

Once partner owns up to a diamond control, you advance via Roman Key-Card Blackwood. His 5♡ response shows two key cards out of five (the four aces and the king of trumps). That is all you need to know. *Being aggressive in the slam zone can bear fruit when you can almost count the requisite tricks.*

♠ A K 9 6 4	YOU	PARTNER
♡ 6	–	1♠
◊ K Q 7 4	?	
♣ K J 3		

When your partner opens the bidding you can immediately contemplate a slam in spades. Your hand contains only five losers and either first- or second-round control in every suit.

If you play 2NT as a game-forcing spade raise, you could try that. Another option you might consider is to start off with a Splinter of 4♡ and follow up with 4NT. However, as you intend to assume captaincy with that second bid, you should not give away any details that might help the opponents find the best defence. Here you plan to bid 7♠ opposite three aces, 6♠ facing two and to stop in five if partner admits to only one. What are you waiting for? Go straight to 4NT to ask him.

♠ 9 5	YOU	PARTNER
♡ A K Q 7 4	–	4♠
◊ A J 10 5	?	
♣ A 3		

Unless you are playing South African Texas (also known as Namyats) you may have a slight doubt about the sort of hand shown by this pre-empt. To be on the safe side, you should mentally place partner with something like K-Q-J-x-x-x-x of spades and a bust, then see how things shape up. Facing that hand your prospects for a slam seem pretty good. At worst the enemy will attack a minor suit in which partner holds two or three small and you will simply require a few rounds of hearts to stand up. At best partner has solid spades and you would want to call a grand slam. In that case you could count thirteen on top if he has either an eighth spade or the heart jack. If not, you might reasonably expect the hearts to ruff out. The only time you want to stay out of a slam is if he has, say, a 7-4 shape with only one of the top three spades. Whatever happens, his response to your 4NT RKCB should enable you to place the contract. *Being aggressive in the slam zone can be right with extra values and good trumps or controls.*

	♠ Q J 10 8 6 4	♠ A K 3
	♡ 7 4	♡ A 10 2
	◊ A J 9	◊ Q 10 8 7 5 2
	♣ A K	♣ J

YOU	RHO	PARTNER	LHO
–	2♡	3◊	Pass
3♠	Pass	4♡	Pass
4NT	Pass	5♣ *	Pass
5NT	Pass	6♠ **	Pass
7♠			

* 0 or 3 key cards (two aces and the trump king)
** No side-suit kings

Earlier in our discussion, we said that you should be wary of bidding a grand slam because doing so jeopardizes your small slam bonus. However, there is a breed of deal, known as a '5 or 7' deal, on which this factor disappears. The one here gives a perfect example. Suppose you were to bid to 6♠. On a heart lead you would win, draw trumps and take a diamond finesse.

If the finesse wins, you can repeat the finesse and eventually throw your heart loser on dummy's long diamonds – making thirteen tricks. On the other hand, if the finesse loses, LHO will cash a heart trick and your small slam will go one down.

Hard though it may be to diagnose these deals, one wants to avoid playing them at the 6-level. Ideally, you call a grand slam or stop in game. ***Being aggressive in the slam zone can turn out well when you will either make five or seven.***

	♠ 3	♠ A K 10 4 2
	♡ A Q J 9 7 6 4	♡ 10
	◊ A 10 6	◊ Q 4
	♣ J 2	♣ A K 8 7 3

Looking at these two hands, a heart slam seems a marginal proposition. If the enemy lead a spade, you will need a 4-3 split to set them up. On an initial club attack you must judge whether to try to ruff that suit good or to play LHO for the club queen.

However, any discussion about possible developments after a black-suit lead ignores how the bidding is likely to have gone. Partner will call both the black suits and you hearts, leaving diamonds as the unbid suit – which means LHO may well lead it. Then, if you guess the diamonds right, you care not how the black suits behave.

Suppose you open 1♡ and hear 1♠ in reply. You are very close to a 3♡ jump rebid, but let us imagine that you content yourself with a simple 2♡. Partner continues with 3♣, and over that you are definitely too good to merely jump to 4♡ – you have semi-solid hearts and, crucially, first-round control of the unbid suit. So, for the moment, you use the fourth suit, 3◊, and go back to 4♡ at your next turn. After that partner seems worth a raise to 5♡, leaving the final decision to you. If the wind is blowing in the right direction, you can advance to 6♡.

♠ K Q J 10 7 5	YOU	PARTNER	♠ 9 4
♡ A K 6	1♠	2♣	♡ J 4
◊ 8 2	3♠	4◊	◊ A K 10 7
♣ A 4	4♡	4♠	♣ K 9 7 6 5
	5♣	5◊	
	6♠		

This time you are clearly strong enough for a jump rebid. Since the bid shows a good 6-card suit or better, 9-x is fine for support and partner makes an advance cue-bid of 4◊ (the fact that he has four diamonds is pure coincidence). You announce your heart control and partner, who has already expressed his values, signs off. Your hand justifies a further slam try (indeed you would have opened an Acol 2♠ or a Benjamin 2♣ if you could), and when this elicits news of the ◊K you jump to the small slam – the 4♠ bid tells you to dismiss any thoughts of seven. Okay, if the defenders start with ace and another trump, you will need clubs 3-3, a squeeze, or both diamond honours onside, but do you really believe that will happen? All the textbooks say to choose an attacking lead against a 6-level suit contract. If you run into an opening trump lead, you can count yourself hard done by. ***Being aggressive in the slam zone can win when the defenders are likely to go wrong.***

♠ A J 7 3 2	YOU	PARTNER	♠ 9 4
♡ K 6	1♠	3◇	♡ A Q
◇ A 6	3♠	3NT	◇ K Q J 10 4 2
♣ Q J 10 4	4◇	4♡	♣ A 9 6
	4♠	5♣	
	5♡	6◇	

On this sequence the opening bid and jump-shift response are clearly marked. If it indicates extra values, you might rebid 3NT, but not everyone plays it that way and it seems safer to make a waiting bid of 3♠ to see what partner does next. In fact he calls 3NT, which denies primary spade support and conveys the semi-balanced nature of his hand. Moreover this indicates stoppers in the two unbid suits, increasing the chance that he has first- or second-round control in them – more good news for slam purposes. Indeed at this point you can feel pretty certain that you are going to reach a slam. You could count yourself unlucky if you caught partner with anything much weaker than what he holds and, despite the duplication in hearts, taking twelve tricks depends on a finesse at worst. In practice, on any lead other than a spade, partner has twelve easy tricks. Even on a spade lead, he can succeed if the club king is onside and sometimes when it is wrong (if spades lie favourably).

Over 3NT, you continue with 4◇, the ace doubleton being perfectly adequate for expressing delayed support. Then comes an exchange of cue-bids. Once partner has cue-bid in both hearts and clubs, you can commit to at least the 6-level. Your 5♡ cue-bid allows partner room to show the king of clubs, but when he cannot do so you give up on the grand slam.

Note that neither of you could safely use 4NT as an enquiry. After partner bid a natural 3NT, a subsequent 4NT by either party would be a sign-off (unless you have a clear agreement to the contrary). *Being aggressive in the slam zone can be prudent when you reckon six is at worst on a finesse.*

On your slam hands the opponents rarely bid much, but when they do some new factors enter the equation. You must consider your defensive potential and the prospect that they may bid even more than they already have.

	♠ 9 7 4	♠ A 6 2	
	♡ 3	♡ 4	
	◇ A J 9 4	◇ K Q 10 8 7 6 2	
	♣ A Q J 6 2	♣ 9 4	

YOU	LHO	PARTNER	RHO
1♣	4♡	5◇	5♡
?			

Although you possess a minimum opening bid in terms of high cards and you know partner may have stretched, there are good reasons for taking the plunge and bidding one more.

For a start, can you feel confident of defeating 5♡? If the opposing diamonds are 2-0 and the ♣K lies on your left, they may rake in eleven easy tricks. Even if the clubs lie favourably for your side, partner may need to find a club lead or switch to ensure a set. Playing IMPs, you can ill afford to risk conceding a double game swing, so you should take out insurance and bid 6◇. With a little luck in the club suit, you will score +1370. Who knows, good old teammates might return with +650/+850 in 5♡-doubled – and that gives a sizeable swing!

Even if you double 5♡ and get it down, how well is a small penalty (probably only +100 or +200) going to score? At pairs, whenever the opponents' 5-level sacrifice costs less than the value of your game, you invariably score poorly for defending because not everyone in the field will go to 5♡ with their cards. Some pairs will be allowed to play 5◇ your way. A small figure in the home column may yield only 20-25% anyway. Advancing to the 6-level when both 6◇ and 5♡ are both going one down therefore costs little – it simply turns a bad result into an awful one. If either contract is making, though, you will fare a great deal better by bidding on. ***Being aggressive in the slam zone can save you from collecting a miserly penalty.***

As we have said, sometimes you cannot find out if partner has the right cards. In chapter 8 we mentioned that in those cases it might be right to take the aggressive action since any winning defence may be hard to find. Both factors apply to our final hand for this chapter, and a new one comes up as well.

	♠ 6		♠ A K Q 9 4
	♡ 5		♡ A 4
	◊ A K Q J 9 6 5 3		◊ 4 2
	♣ Q 10 6		♣ J 8 4 2

YOU	LHO	PARTNER	RHO
–	3♡	3♠	4♡
?			

Here partner might have the right hand to make 6◊ cold, but in fact he does not. Even so, LHO may lead a heart, which will allow you to pitch two clubs on the spades and still make 6◊.

There is also a third way that a leap to slam can gain over a simple 5◊ bid, particularly if only your side is vulnerable. Might not one of the defenders then sacrifice in 6♡? In this type of auction, one stands a fair chance of bouncing the opponents into a 6-level save. *Being aggressive in the slam zone can result in the enemy taking a phantom sacrifice.*

Golden Rule Nine:

Being Conservative in the Slam Zone can

. . . Protect your game bonus;
. . . Protect your small slam bonus (when thinking of seven);
. . . Save you from going down in a slam try;
. . . Avoid a low-scoring game at pairs;
. . . Let you zap an opposing part-score at rubber or Chicago.

Being Aggressive in the Slam Zone can

. . . Be okay if you have a part-score at rubber or Chicago;
. . . Bear fruit when you can almost count the requisite tricks;
. . . Be right with extra values and good trumps or controls;
. . . Turn out well when you will make either five or seven;
. . . Win when the defenders are likely to go wrong;
. . . Be prudent when you reckon six is at worst on a finesse;
. . . Save you from collecting a miserly penalty;
. . . Result in the enemy taking a phantom sacrifice.

Rule Ten: Stay Low on a Misfit

Nobody relishes a misfit. Partner bids your shortage and he does not like your suits. Sometimes you both have two-suited hands, with no overlap. Hands with great-looking potential fizzle out to almost nothing and various hazards await you in the play. For example, if dummy has few cards in both trumps and a side suit, the defenders can play a round or two of trumps and then cash winners in dummy's other shortage.

On occasion, playing in no-trumps offers a solution to a misfit hand, but communications frequently prove problematic. You set up plenty of winners in one hand but the defenders lock you in the other. Indeed, you will often score fewer tricks than you would with two balanced hands facing each other.

	YOU	PARTNER	
♠ Q 8 6 5 2			♠ J 4
♡ 3 2	–	1♡	♡ K J 8 6 4
◇ 7 4	1♠	2◇	◇ A K 6 2
♣ A K Q 4	?		♣ 5 3

With 11 HCP and close to an opening bid yourself, perhaps you feel tempted to try 2NT now?

To do so would be sheer slavery to point count. Partner has shown at least nine red cards, and, as he might have raised spades at his second turn with 3-card support, he is likely to be short there. If you bid 2NT and find him with, say, 14 HCP, he will raise you to game. From where do you imagine that nine tricks might come?

The best policy is to give simple preference to 2♡. Indeed, nobody can underwrite even that modest contract. You must hope partner can score a few high-card tricks and scramble some trump winners to bring his tally to eight. *Staying low on a misfit can let you stop in a making contract.*

Good players listen hard to the bidding for sounds of a misfit. If they detect their opponents going overboard and the cards lying badly, they will freely apply a penalty double to a game contract. Make sure you do not fall into such a trap.

♠ K 10 2	YOU	PARTNER	♠ A 6 4
♡ A K J 9 4	1♡	2♣	♡ 6
◇ J 9 7 2	2◇	3♣	◇ Q 3
♣ 4	?		♣ Q J 8 7 6 5 2

Assuming you do not play a 2/1 response as forcing to game (in which case partner would obviously have responded 1NT), are you thinking of making another bid because you dislike partner's suit? After all, you have a solid spade stopper and, if you can make nine tricks playing in a suit where you hold a singleton, then surely you stand a chance in no-trumps . . .

This is the type of muddled thinking that leads to four-figure penalties. Do you really want to play 3NT-doubled on these two hands? *Staying low on a misfit can avoid your conceding a doubled penalty.*

On most misfit hands, neither side can make much. Still, if you stop low enough, you may entice your opponents into the auction, allowing you to go plus by defending.

♠ A 10 6 4	YOU	PARTNER	♠ J 5 2
♡ K J 7 3	–	1♣	♡ A 6
◇ Q 8 6 4 2	1◇	2♣	◇ K 7
♣ –	?		♣ K Q 10 7 4 2

When you responded 1◇ to partner's opening bid you hoped that he would rebid in one of the majors. That would have given you a reasonable fit and increased the chance of game. In fact he bids your void again – hardly what you wanted to hear.

There is no point introducing a major at this juncture as partner has denied them and, although you possess stoppers in the other suits, you must refrain from bidding 2NT. Such a bid would invite game, which you surely do not want to do. Your void will hinder partner in setting up his clubs and you can offer no source of tricks yourself. A much better strategy is to pass, preferably in tempo. Many opponents cannot bear to defend a low-level contract and, if they enter the auction, you might well manage to extract a juicy penalty. *Staying low on a misfit can give the opponents a chance to come in and go down.*

♠ K 9 7 6 5 2	YOU	PARTNER	♠ –
♡ –	–	1♡	♡ A J 8 4 3
◇ 9 6 4 3	1♠	2♣	◇ A 8 2
♣ 8 6 4			♣ A 9 5 3 2

You have done well to extricate yourselves from playing in your side's worst fit. However, it would be gilding the lily to repeat your spades or indeed to take any positive action. Your hand will surely contribute much more as dummy in a club contract than it would have done in 1♡. If you try any heroics, you risk losing the benefit of your earlier decision to keep the bidding open. *Staying low on a misfit can allow you to benefit from an earlier decision.*

Of course you cannot stop on every misfitting hand. On occasion you can make game or find a better strain to play in:

♠ Q	YOU	PARTNER	♠ A K 8 7 4 2
♡ A K 7 6 4	1♡	1♠	♡ 5
◇ K Q J 9	2◇	2♠	◇ 10 6 4
♣ K 10 3	?		♣ Q 7 2

You cannot claim much in the way of support for partner's suit, but this time you have genuine extra values and game aspirations opposite anything more than a minimum. You are certainly worth another effort, but a jump to game would seem overly optimistic.

You have two choices of invitational actions – 2NT and 3♠. Many players would take one look at their singleton spade and bid no-trumps, but doing so could well rebound. Think about how you can expect the play to go . . .

Well, needless to say, communication problems are likely to wreck your chances in a no-trump game. Whilst partner has warned that his hand may have little to offer unless spades are trumps, you should see the potential of your singleton queen in a spade contract. Raise to 3♠ – on his actual hand, partner will be delighted to accept the invitation and on normal breaks he should manage to score ten tricks with consummate ease. *Do not stay low on a misfit when you have real extra values.*

♠	—	YOU	PARTNER	♠ K J 8 6 5 2
♡	Q J 10 9 8 7 4	—	1♠	♡ 6
◇	K 4 3	2♡	2♠	◇ A 6 5
♣	Q J 2	?		♣ K 10 4

Yes, this looks like a misfit. Even so, do you honestly think partner wants to struggle away in 2♠? He has hardly promised a tremendous suit, and the solidity of your hearts suggests that the hand will play better in that strain, even if partner turns up with a void. As the cards lie, taking nine tricks with hearts as trumps should prove more or less routine. *Do not stay low on a misfit when your suit should play better than partner's.*

♠ K Q 8 6 5 2	YOU	PARTNER	♠ 4 3
♡ 6	—	1♡	♡ K Q 9 7 3
◇ Q J 6	1♠	2♣	◇ 10 4
♣ 9 7 4	2♠		♣ A K 3 2

Your realistic choices at your second turn are to pass 2♣ or to rebid your spade suit. Neither comes with any guarantees, and one can readily construct hands for partner where it will work best for you to simply put down the dummy. However, the odds appear high that 2♠ will provide a better spot.

We hope you can see another reason for advancing to 2♠ on this collection. Your hand is not terrible and, if you find partner with the right cards, he might raise and game could make. Perhaps he has something like:

> ♠ A 3
> ♡ A 8 7 5 2
> ◇ 5
> ♣ A K J 10 2

His superb controls and partial spade support probably justify raising 2♠ to game. On certain layouts Four Spades might go down, but you would surely want to try for it. You will never get there by passing 2♣. *Do not stay low on a misfit when same level correction ought to improve matters.*

♠ K 9 7 4	YOU	PARTNER	♠ A 3
♡ K 9 8 5 2	–	1♢	♡ 10
♢ 10 3	1♡	3♣	♢ A K Q J 2
♣ 10 2	3NT		♣ A J 9 7 4

Even though this hand may look like a misfit, it is highly dangerous to randomly pass when partner has made a forcing bid. Whilst doing so may bring you a beneficial result on an individual deal, the resulting damage to partnership confidence will lead to numerous future losses. If partner forces, assume he knows what he is doing and keep bidding. Do not attempt to second-guess partner: he can see his hand while you cannot. ***Do not stay low on a misfit when partner's bid is forcing.***

Golden Rule Ten:

Staying Low on a Misfit can

. . . Let you stop in a making contract;
. . . Avoid your conceding a doubled penalty;
. . . Give the opponents a chance to come in and go down;
. . . Allow you to benefit from an earlier decision.

Do not Stay Low on a Misfit when

. . . You have real extra values;
. . . Your suit should play better than partner's;
. . . Same level correction ought to improve matters;
. . . Partner's bid is forcing.

Rule Eleven: Select Your Best Fit as Trumps

We started chapter 1 with an observation that trumps take tricks, and we end by repeating this advice. Other things being equal, a fit consisting of eight cards or better should provide a reasonable spot in which to play. Trumps can serve as winners in their own right, but they also help stop the enemy suit and with setting up side suits. Moreover, by ruffing in the short trump hand, they often enable you to take extra tricks. As usual we begin with examples of when you should follow the rule:

♠ A Q 10 9 5 3	YOU	PARTNER	♠ K J
♡ A 8 4	1♠	2♢	♡ 6
♢ 6	2♠	3♣	♢ A J 9 3 2
♣ 10 7 5	3♡	3♠	♣ Q J 8 6 2
	4♠		

Although you have all suits stopped, spades is clearly better than no-trumps. On a heart lead or switch 3NT will surely fail. In 4♠ you mean to ruff two hearts in dummy or, if LHO leads a trump, you can ruff one heart and eventually set up a club.

♠ K J 6	YOU	PARTNER	♠ A Q 10 4 2
♡ A Q 10 6 2	–	1♠	♡ K J 5
♢ A Q 5	2♡	3♡	♢ 9 7 4 3
♣ 9 7	3♠	4♡	♣ K
	5♢	5NT	
	6♡		

The early rounds of bidding uncover your side's major-suit fits and slam potential, and partner's 'pick a slam' 5NT asks you to decide. With spades as trumps you cannot productively ruff anything and all depends on the diamond finesse. The fact that you have no singleton should enable you to foresee this. You should choose hearts as trumps, where a club ruff gives the twelfth trick. *Selecting your best fit as trumps can make extra ruffing winners possible.*

♠ K J 7 4	YOU	PARTNER	♠ A Q 9 6
♡ 6 3	–	1NT	♡ 8 4
◇ A J 7	2♣	2♠	◇ K Q 10 5
♣ A K 10 2	4♠		♣ Q J 3

When partner opens with a weak (12-14 HCP) 1NT, you expect to be able to make game. 3NT will coast home opposite most balanced hands, but you should constantly watch out for exceptions, particularly if partner's weakness matches yours, as it does here. You should therefore investigate a 4-4 spade fit via Stayman – you can always settle for 3NT at your second turn if partner does not hold four spades.

Looking at the two hands, you can count twelve effortless tricks in 3NT. The only slight problem is that the opponents can cash at least five heart winners before you ever gain the lead! Playing in spades, they can score no more than two hearts.

When we talk about a fit we typically mean a trump suit of eight cards or better – you may recall from chapter 10 that only seven trumps is normally a misfit. If you have a 4-4 fit, then, on a normal 3-2 break, you can draw the enemy trumps and still have one left in each hand to make independently.

With a 5-3 fit the position remains good, but differs slightly. As a 4-3-3-3 pattern is not the norm, you can expect a dummy with three trumps still to offer a ruffing value. Also, now the long trumps consist of five cards, you have the potential to accept a force and draw trumps even if there is a 4-1 break. Whilst 6-2 and 7-1 fits offer less scope for ruffing in the short hand, they confer other benefits, as we shall see.

If the best fit between the two hands comprises just seven cards, you will often prefer to play in no-trumps. The times when you do better in a suit usually occur when the trump suit is solid or nearly so. Also, 6-1 and 5-2 fits generally play better than a 4-3. In fact a 4-3 fit tends to work well only when the defenders cannot force the 4-card holding to ruff. This happens either if the 3-trump hand has the shortage in the enemy long suit or if you have loads of high cards.

One of the most frequent reasons for choosing to play in a suit contract rather than no-trumps is the ability to stop the opponents from cashing too many tricks in their long suit.

♠ 10 4		♠ A K Q J 6
♡ 7 5 4 3		♡ 6 2
◊ A 10 7		◊ K Q 5
♣ A 9 3 2		♣ K 6 4

YOU	LHO	PARTNER	RHO
–	–	–	1♡
Pass	Pass	Double	Pass
2♣	Pass	2♠	Pass
3♡	Pass	3♠	Pass
4♠			

After doubling first, partner introduces his suit at his second turn, which promises quite a strong hand. You want to play in game, but which one is unclear. So you cue-bid RHO's suit. Once partner denies a stopper by failing to bid 3NT, you settle for the most likely game – 4♠. *Selecting your best fit as trumps can enable you to stop the opponent's suit.*

♠ A Q 10 6	YOU	PARTNER	♠ K J 8 4
♡ A	–	1NT	♡ J 10 5
◊ K J 10 7 5 4	2NT	3◊	◊ Q 9 6
♣ K J	3♠	4♠	♣ A Q 5
	4NT	5♡	
	6◊		

1NT is 12-14 and 2NT is a transfer to diamonds. Partner's 3◊ indicates a fitting honour in the suit. With no support he would bid 3♣, although some people play it the other way round. Partner then raises your 3♠ to game. This suits you nicely as you can use RKCB to ask about aces and the ♠K. His 5♡ reply promises two of the three missing key cards.

Partner has done nothing to suggest the ♡K, so you clearly want to choose a suit slam. Although a 4-4 fit can provide better offensive ruffing potential than a 6-3 fit, here the decisive factor is the danger of an adverse ruff. Whilst a 3-1 diamond break will often defeat 6♠, a 4-1 spade division can only beat 6◊ if someone has four spades and the ◊A. *Selecting your best fit as trumps can avoid you having your long suit ruffed.*

♠ K 10 3	YOU	PARTNER	♠ A J 6
♡ A 4	–	1♢	♡ 10 2
♢ K 10 9 3	2NT *	3♢	♢ A Q J 8 6 5
♣ A K 7 2	4♢	4♠ **	♣ J 3
	5♣ **	5♢	
	6♢		

* Baron, 16+
** cue-bid

Playing in a suit contract gives you many more options in the play. If you had bid this pair of hands to 6NT, you would win the first or second round of hearts and eventually have to guess which defender held the ♠Q. Even supposing that you are a very good guesser, you would sometimes go down.

Six diamonds, on the other hand, is 100% unless you run into an untimely ruff. You can win the opening heart lead, draw trumps, eliminate the clubs, and exit with the second round of hearts. The defenders will then have to either lead a spade, solving your guess in that suit, or give you a ruff and discard, thus allowing you to pitch your third spade. *Selecting your best fit as trumps can allow you to strip the hand.*

♠ 10 7	YOU	PARTNER	♠ A K Q 5 3
♡ 7 5 4 2	–	1♠	♡ K 6
♢ A 10 2	1NT	3♢	♢ K Q 9 4
♣ K J 5 2	4♠		♣ Q 7

Partner is just too weak to open 2NT and, in any case, many people would shy away from opening that with a 5-4-2-2 type. Unfortunately your 1NT response means any no-trump contract would get played from the wrong side of the table. Clearly you cannot bid 3NT at your second turn since partner might have a singleton heart. Nor is there any point temporising with 3♠. Your heart weakness warns against any attempt to declare the hand and partner's next action may give away vital information about his shape. Even if your RHO manages to find a safe lead against 4♠, he may have an awkward guess if partner plays a low club towards the king-jack. Sometimes going in with the ace will be right but here it sets up the suit. *Selecting your best fit as trumps can keep strength and shape concealed.*

♠ A K 9	YOU	PARTNER	♠ Q 8 6 3 2
♡ A 5	–	Pass	♡ 8 2
◇ 4 3 2	1♣	2♠	◇ A 8
♣ K Q 8 5 2	3♡	3NT	♣ A 10 6 3
	4♣	4◇	
	6♣		

Whether or not you are playing fit-showing jumps in other situations, a jump in a new suit by a passed hand always shows support for your suit and five or more cards in the suit bid. If you have opened a major, partner should have a source of tricks, but when you call a minor he sometimes needs to introduce a raggedy major since game in it might be best.

Your 3♡ initially indicates heart values whilst creating a game force, and you quickly find out that partner has a stopper in diamonds that is also a control. Partner cannot really have the same high cards and a 6-1-2-4 shape because then he would have an opening bid. So you dismiss thoughts of a grand and pick the safest small slam. With clubs as trumps you can overcome any 4-1 spade split by ruffing out the suit. *Selecting your best fit as trumps can permit you to ruff a suit good.*

♠ A K 8	YOU	PARTNER	♠ 9 6 3
♡ A	–	2♡	♡ K Q J 10 8 2
◇ A 8 7 6 4	2NT	3♡	◇ J 5
♣ A 10 3 2	4♡		♣ 9 7

As it happens your side has two 7-card fits although at the table you would not know where the other one is. In any case, if partner pre-empts in one suit, you need something a great deal better than A-x-x-x-x to consider playing in your suit.

You enquire with 2NT and we assume that partner's reply announces a minimum hand but a good suit. Surely this is all you need to know. How can you possibly reach his hand in 3NT? If instead of answering about range and suit quality, you give features over 2NT, you get to the same position. The fact that partner has no outside features to show means his trumps must be good. *Selecting your best fit as trumps can provide an entry to the long suit.*

	YOU	PARTNER	♠ A K 7 4
♠ —	1♣	1♡	♡ K 6 5 3
♡ Q 7 2	2◇	2♠	◇ J 10 4
◇ A K 8 6	3♣	4♣	♣ K 10
♣ A Q J 9 7 5	4◇	4♠	
	5♣	5♡	
	6♣		

Playing in a suit can increase your options in the play in other ways, too. Suppose you were in 6NT on a spade lead. You could win the opening lead in dummy, but the discard from your hand helps little.

Playing in clubs, you are not forced to play a high spade at trick one, which improves your chances significantly. Suppose you ruff the spade lead and lead a heart towards dummy. If LHO holds the ace, he has a choice of losing options. If he takes his ace, you will have two heart tricks – your diamond losers can then go away on dummy's high spades after you have drawn trumps. If LHO ducks his ♡A, you can throw your two remaining hearts on the high spades and subsequently concede a diamond trick.

If RHO holds the ♡A, you will pitch one loser from each red suit on dummy's spade winners and later take the diamond finesse for your contract. You may still go down this way, but your chances are much better than they are in 6NT, where you must stake everything on the diamond finesse. *Selecting your best fit as trumps can keep discard options open.*

♠ A K Q J 10	YOU	PARTNER	♠ 8 6
♡ K 9 5	–	1NT	♡ A Q 8 4
◇ Q J 4	?		◇ K 10 2
♣ 8 6			♣ Q J 9 5

At rubber bridge, Chicago and in certain other competitions (the Hubert Phillips for example) honours count: 100 for four of the top five trumps and 150 for all five. Hearing partner open a weak no-trump you feel confident about game. So you choose the highest-scoring strain, in this case spades. *Selecting your best fit as trumps can let you claim honours.*

You will recall that we said earlier you normally want to play in an 8-card fit. The exception comes with minor-suit games. The scoring table means that you need to take eleven tricks in order to make game in clubs or diamonds. So, merely to break even, you need to score two more tricks with a minor suit as trumps than in no-trumps. This rarely happens unless you have a suit wide-open or big trump fit. Even with one suit unstopped you may still fare better in 3NT. If you have three low facing three low in one suit, that is three top losers, which could spell instant defeat for 5♣/♦. On the other hand, if that suit breaks 4-3 and everything else is solid, you might still make 3NT. When you do have something in every suit you very often want to play in 3NT.

♠ 10 9	YOU	PARTNER	♠ Q J 8 7
♡ K 10 5	1♦	1♠	♡ J
◊ A Q J 10 8 3	2♦	3♡	◊ K 9 6 4 2
♣ K 10	3NT		♣ A J 9

It seems pretty obvious, but nine tricks really are easier to take than eleven. Despite an 11-card diamond fit on this deal, bidding to game in that suit would produce a poor result as the defenders have three top winners to take. However, they can never prevent from you taking nine tricks in no-trumps. When partner makes a 3♡ Splinter you can work out that your ♡K will be useful in 3NT but probably worthless in 5◊.

♠ J 9	YOU	PARTNER	♠ A 7
♡ J 7 3	–	1NT	♡ Q 6 5 2
◊ A K Q 9 5 3 2		3NT	◊ J 10 6 4
♣ 2			♣ A Q 7

Again you have an 11-card fit, and once more the diamond game represents a very poor proposition. Even if the defenders cannot score a heart ruff, you will need to find a favourable lie in the heart suit in order to avoid three natural losers. Also you will need the club finesse to work. By contrast, taking nine tricks in no-trumps is trivial. ***Do not select your best fit as trumps when nine tricks are easier than eleven.***

Sometimes the solution to having insufficient winners for five of a minor and too few stoppers for 3NT is to play in a major. This tends to be where the 4-3 fit (sometimes referred to as Moysian fit after Alphonse Moyse) comes into its own. In fact one can construct hands on which you actually want to choose a trump suit in which the enemy trumps outnumber yours.

♠ A Q J 7	YOU	PARTNER	♠ K 9 2
♡ A K 5	1♠	2◇	♡ 10 3
◇ 10 9 6 3	2NT	3◇	◇ A J 8 7 4 2
♣ Q 2	3♡	3♠	♣ J 5
	3NT	4♠	

This is a particularly difficult deal and pairs using a strong no-trump opening have virtually no chance. On the other hand, if you play 4-card majors and a weak no-trump, you might manage to avoid the hopeless games in both the 10-card minor and no-trumps.

Here, you force to game with a 15+ HCP 2NT rebid and partner discloses his extra diamond length. When you then show heart values (implying club weakness) on the way to 3NT, partner knows that the 9-trick game is the wrong spot and he corrects to spades.

Once in a blue moon, you may encounter a deal on which even a 4-2 major-suit fit will be the only making game, although bidding to the top spot on such a layout is incredibly tough. Still, you can sometimes do it, as the next deal illustrates:

♠ A K Q J	YOU	PARTNER	♠ 10 2
♡ 8 5	–	3◇	♡ J 3
◇ 6 3	3♠	4♠	◇ A J 9 8 7 4 2
♣ A K Q J 2	Pass		♣ 10 5

When partner opens 3◇ it seems unlikely that you want to play in 5♣. By responding 3♠ you give him the chance to rebid 3NT with something in hearts. He cannot do that, but a whiff of spade support is music to your ears. Dummy can ruff hearts and you just need spades 4-3. *Do not select your best fit as trumps when only playing in a major lets you score game.*

Over the last couple of pages we have discussed how the difficulties in making the eleven tricks required for game in a minor has impacted your choice of trump suit. However, it is probably at the slam level that choosing the correct trump suit assumes paramount importance. We have previously advised you to avoid bidding weak suits on possible slam hands. Apart from the fact that partners tend to assume you have a control in any suit you mention, you must be very wary of ending up in the wrong suit. A lengthy trump suit with a gaping hole in it is useless in a slam. Defenders may lose side-suit tricks if they fail to attack the right suit at trick one, but their trump winners hardly ever run away. Therefore, in any slam decision, you must consider the solidity of the potential trump suit.

♠ K 9 2	YOU	PARTNER	♠ A 8 7 5 4 3
♡ K	–	1♠	♡ A J 5
◇ K 9 3	3♣	3♠	◇ A 8 7
♣ A K Q J 10 4	4NT	5♣	♣ 5
	5◇	5♠	
	7♣		

A grand slam that requires a 2-2 break is a poor proposition, and 7♠ needs trumps to divide evenly. By contrast, playing in clubs, you need little more than spades not to split 4-0. Having won a possible diamond lead with the king and drawn trumps, you can discard the third spade from your hand on dummy's ♡A and then ruff the suit good for a diamond discard.

On both sides of the Atlantic, Roman Key-Card Blackwood has virtually displaced the traditional 4NT simple ace ask as the norm. This deal provides a perfect example of it in action: you ask for key-cards with 4NT and partner confirms that he holds the three missing aces. When you then ask about the queen of trumps (spades at this point, as that was the last suit bid), he denies possessing that card. *Do not select your best fit as trumps when playing in a solid suit avoids a trump loser.*

On that hand the potential weak spot in your side's longest trump suit was fairly obvious. Sometimes you need to picture how the play will go in order to realise the problem.

♠ K Q 6	YOU	PARTNER	♠ A 10 5
♡ A K Q 10 4	2♣	2♢	♡ J 5
♢ 9	2♡	3NT	♢ Q 8 7 4
♣ A K Q J	4♣	4♠	♣ 7 5 3 2
	5NT	6♡	

As RKCB enables you to find out about the king and queen of trumps, you no longer need 5NT for that purpose. Instead, many pairs use 5NT to ask partner to 'pick-a-slam'. This deal demonstrates how useful this can be. Partner promises values with his jump to 3NT and he then cue-bids spades to show his club fit. Your jump to 5NT then asks him to choose between hearts and clubs. Having denied any kind of heart fit earlier in the auction, he could hardly produce much better support, while his clubs are anaemic.

He therefore chooses hearts, which is a much safer slam if the defenders start off with two rounds of diamonds. Playing in clubs, you would have to ruff with one of your high trumps and a 4-1 trump split would then sink the contract. With hearts as trumps, the same defence would prevail only if someone holds five trumps. *Do not select your best fit as trumps when doing so means ruffing high.*

♠ A J 3	YOU	PARTNER	♠ K Q 10 9 7 5 2
♡ A 8 7 5	–	3♠	♡ 9 4
♢ J 10 6 2	?		♢ 8 4
♣ A 5			♣ J 3

Nearly always, A-J-x will suffice to play for no loser opposite a suit that can be opened at the 3-level. So you can bid 3NT. This decision is closer at match-point scoring – if, say, partner has three clubs, a ruff in the short trump hand will give you ten tricks. Conversely, at IMPs or rubber bridge, the decision is clear cut – you can virtually count nine tricks in no-trumps. With partner's hand as shown here, you can make exactly the same nine tricks playing in spades. Many players would simply raise to 4♠ because it would not occur to them to call 3NT with such good support. Needless to say, once you spot the possibility of running nine fast tricks, you should act on it.

♠ A K J 7 4	YOU	PARTNER	♠ Q 8 6
♡ Q 10 2	–	1♣	♡ J 9 5
◇ J 9 6	1♠	1NT	◇ Q 7
♣ K 4	3NT		♣ A Q J 10 2

On this occasion we assume partner is in a strong no-trump position. No doubt you could look for a 5-3 spade fit over 1NT, probably via a Crowhurst 2♣ (in Acol) or Checkback 2◇ (with Standard American). Jumping to 3◇ would give another way to do it if neither of these options are available to you. However, you need to appreciate that partner might have already supported your spades with three if the rest of his hand appeared suitable. Remember, he knows that your space-consuming 1♠ response would often be based on a 5-card suit. The fact that he chose 1NT may well indicate that his hand looks a bit like yours, with secondary red-suit honours.

With these hands one might also reach the best contract with you as the dealer. Then the auction 1♠-2♣-2♠-3♣-3NT would be very reasonable. *Do not select your best fit as trumps when you can run the same tricks in no-trumps.*

♠ Q 8 7 6 5	YOU	PARTNER	♠ A K 3
♡ A K 7	1♠	2♡	♡ Q 8 5 4 2
◇ K 8	2NT	3♠	◇ Q 10 3
♣ A Q 9	4♣	5♣	♣ K 6
	6NT		

On this deal, you have a choice of 8-card major-suit fits. By eschewing them both and choosing to play in no-trumps, you significantly improve your chances. One can easily see why.

With spades as trumps, the slam depends on trumps 3-2. Similarly, a 3-2 trump split will also be required if you play in hearts. Playing the deal in no-trumps enables you to combine those two chances – you will make 12 tricks if *either* major divides evenly. Indeed, even if both key suits break 4-1, you may have squeeze chances if one defender has four cards in each major. *Do not select your best fit as trumps when you need one of two suits to break.*

	♠ A Q J 10		♠ K 8 6 4
	♡ K Q 10 4 2		♡ A 9 7 3
	◊ A K 5		◊ J 8 4
	♣ 6		♣ Q 10

YOU	LHO	PARTNER	RHO
–	3♣	Pass	Pass
Double	Pass	4♣	Pass
5♣	Pass	5♡	Pass
6♠			

The jump to 6♠ is hard to find and even some experts would miss it. As you can see, you would need the ◊Q to fall to make 6♡. Assuming an even trump split, you can make an extra trick in spades as partner's third diamond can go on your long heart. You will then be able to score your twelfth trick with a ruff.

When you have a choice between a strong 4-4 fit and a trump suit with nine cards, it will frequently pay to make the 4-4 fit trumps. *Do not select your best fit as trumps when you require a discard on the long card.*

♠ K 9 4 3	YOU	PARTNER	♠ A Q 10 8 7 5
♡ K 7 2	–	1♠	♡ 8 6
◊ A Q J 9 7 5	3◊	3♠	◊ K
♣ –	4♣	4◊	♣ K 7 5 2
	?		

Once you have agreed a trump suit, it is often difficult to play then in a different suit. On this deal, you need to avoid exposing the ♡K to a potentially disastrous opening lead.

Your initial jump-shift response suggested either very strong diamonds or a two-suited hand with diamonds and spades. Then 4♣ confirmed both the spade fit and a club control and partner cue-bid in diamonds. This must show the king, as he should not make an early cue-bid in your suit with a shortage.

If you were to continue cue-bidding now, it would be virtually impossible to avoid playing in spades – partner will view a later 6◊ bid as a grand slam try. If, however, you jump straight to 6◊, partner should work out why you have done so, and pass.

	YOU	PARTNER	
♠ K 8			♠ 6 5
♡ 10 3	–	1◊	♡ A J 2
◊ K 8 2	2♣	3◊	◊ A Q J 9 7 3
♣ A Q J 10 7 2	4◊	4♡	♣ K 6
	4♠	5♣	
	5NT	6NT	

On this sequence you quickly find out that partner has better than minimum values and a good six-card diamond suit. Then on the next two rounds you hear that he has controls in hearts and clubs. Your ♠K-x may face low cards – bad news for 6◊ – so you give partner a choice of slams with 5NT. As neither of his cue-bids were shortages, he calls 6NT. *Do not select your best fit as trumps when you have to protect a tenace.*

	YOU	PARTNER	
♠ K J 6 4 3			♠ A Q 10 8
♡ –	–	1♣	♡ A K 4
◊ K Q J 10 8 5	1◊	1NT	◊ 6 4
♣ A J	2♠	3♡	♣ K 10 9 3
	4♣	4♡	
	5♠	6♠	
	6NT		

As a matter of style some people might bid opener's hand differently, but you should still be able to learn certain key things. These are that partner is 15-16 balanced, has primary spade support and both first- and second-round heart control.

6◊ and 6♠ are each reasonable contracts – both will make more often than they fail. Even so, the defenders stand to profit from bad breaks more often than one would like. A 4-1 diamond split (where the ace is not singleton) will enable the enemy to score a ruff to beat 6♠. Likewise, if the defender with the ◊A also holds three spades, then a spade lead and later ruff will put paid to 6◊ (assuming the defender with one spade has more than one diamond). Diamonds 5-0 may beat both slams.

Playing the hand in no-trumps often allows you to overcome unfavourable distribution – there is no trump suit to break badly and no unexpected ruff to avoid. *Do not select your best fit as trumps when an adverse ruff could beat you.*

We conclude with a couple of hands on which the precise scoring method in use determines the winning action.

♠ 10 5	YOU	PARTNER	♠ A J 4
♡ Q J 7 5	–	1♦	♡ K 6
◊ K 9 6 4	1♡	1NT	◊ A Q 7 3 2
♣ 10 6 2	Pass		♣ Q 8 4

For sure 2◊ looks safer, certainly from seeing only your own hand, but at match-point scoring you have to do without such luxuries. You can ill afford to make +90/110 in diamonds when the majority of other pairs holding your cards are chalking up +120 in 1NT. Of course, the defensive cards will occasionally lie very poorly, and then 1NT will go down while you make 2◊. Needless to say, playing for the odd success represents poor match-point tactics.

An added reason for stopping in 1NT is that the opponents are much less likely to back into the auction. If you remove partner to 2◊, your RHO might well balance and then you could find yourselves defending 2♠ – a decidedly unfriendly development. *Do not select your best fit as trumps when it is a minor at match-points.*

♠ A 9 7	YOU	PARTNER	♠ J 3
♡ A J 9 7 4	–	Pass	♡ K 10 3
◊ A J 8	1♡	2◊	◊ K Q 10 7 2
♣ A J	3NT		♣ 10 5 3

When using a scoring method in which honours count, do not forget that four aces in no-trumps scores 150. Here, facing a passed partner, game appears safe but chances of a slam remote. So you can afford to bash 3NT. The extra 150 points should more than offset any overtricks you might lose. In any case, almost half of the time the enemy will lead a club, giving you ample time to develop the hearts. Even if they do find the spade lead, they will have several discards to make and they may well throw so many spades away that you can safely take a heart finesse. *Do not select your best fit as trumps when your four aces count as honours.*

Golden Rule Eleven:

Selecting Your Best Fit as Trumps can

. . . Make extra ruffing winners possible;
. . . Enable you to stop the opponent's long suit;
. . . Avoid your having long suit ruffed;
. . . Allow you to strip the hand;
. . . Keep shape and strength concealed;
. . . Permit you to ruff a suit good;
. . . Provide an entry to the long suit;
. . . Keep discard options open;
. . . Let you claim honours.

Do not Select Your Best Fit as Trumps when

. . . Nine tricks are easier than eleven;
. . . Only playing in a major lets you score game;
. . . Doing so means ruffing high;
. . . Playing in a solid suit avoids a loser;
. . . You can run the same tricks in no-trumps;
. . . You need one of two suits to break;
. . . You require a discard on the long card;
. . . You have to protect a tenace;
. . . An adverse ruff could beat you;
. . . It is a minor at match-points;
. . . When your four aces count as honours.